**Professional English**

# English for Business

Josephine O'Brien

**THOMSON**

**HEINLE**

Australia • Canada • México • Singapore • United Kingdom • United States

**THOMSON**

**HEINLE**

# English for Business

Josephine O'Brien

**Publisher, Global ELT:** Christopher Wenger
**Director of Content Development:** Anita Raducanu
**Director of Product Marketing:** Amy Mabley
**Editorial Manager:** Berta de Llano
**International Marketing Manager:** Ian Martin
**Development Editor:** Margarita Matte, Ivor Williams
**Editorial Assistant:** Jason Seigel
**Production Editor:** John Sarantakis

**Photo Researcher:** Alejandra Camarillo
**Illustrator:** Ignacio (Iñaki) Ochoa Bilbao
**Interior Design/Composition:** Miriam Gómez Alvarado
**Cover Design:** Miriam Gómez Alvarado
**Printer:** Webcom

For more information contact Thomson Heinle,
25 Thomson Place, Boston, Massachusetts 02210 USA,
or visit our Internet site at elt.thomson.com

For permission to use material from this text or product,
submit a request online at http://www.thomsonrights.com

Any additional questions about permissions can be
submitted by email to thomsonrights@thomson.com

**ISBN 13:** 978-1-4130-2050-2
**ISBN 10:** 1-4130-2050-X

Library of Congress Control Number
2007920379

**Cover Photo Credits:**
TR: © Design Pics Inc. / Alamy; all other photos: © Comstock Images /
Alamy.

**Photo Credits:**
p. 2 © Comstock Images / Alamy, p. 32 © Jack Sullivan / Alamy, p. 34 ©
Carlos Davila / Alamy, p. 36 © Content Mine International / Alamy, p. 57
© Comstock Images / Alamy, p. 62 © Comstock Images / Alamy All other
photos (c) photos.com

# Contents

# To the Teacher

**English for Business** is especially designed for university students at the intermediate level who want to use their English for international communication in professional contexts.

## Objective

The purpose of this book is to empower students with the language and life skills they need to carry out their career goals. To this end it provides ample opportunities for students to build awareness and practice the language in real-life scenarios. Its integrated skills approach develops the student's self-confidence to survive and succeed in professional and social encounters within an English-speaking global community.

## Content

The book has been designed with a core of 30 lessons plus additional resource sections to provide teachers and course designers with the necessary flexibility for planning a wide variety of courses.

The four skills of listening, speaking, writing and reading are developed throughout each unit within professional contexts. Emphasis is on developing the life skills students need to deal with situations that they will encounter in the job market.

University students, regardless of their major, will immediately be motivated by the opportunity to prepare for the job market as they practice their English language skills in the following scenarios.

### Preparing for the Job Market

reading and discussing job advertisments, looking at the functions of the HR department, form filling and resume preparation, e-mailing and interview procedures

### Sales Issues

describing the characteristics of a good salesperson, analyzing different sales situations, customer relations and dealing with customer complaints, preparing sales presentations, analyzing Internet sales

### Marketing Products and Plans

describing products and brands and analyzing appeal to customers, creating marketing plans, conducting meetings, presenting copyright issues

### Finance and Economics

discussing financial issues, managing personal expenses, opening a bank account, managing business expenses, describing economic issues that affect business, describing investment options including online finance

### Global Concerns in Business

analyzing cultural differences in business deals, describing a variety of corporate cultures, analyzing the changing face of the workplace, discussing global issues that affect the business world

## Using the Book

Each content-based unit is divided into six two-page lessons. Each lesson is designed to present, develop and practice job-related skills. (See **Content**.)

## Vocabulary

A section with additional content vocabulary for Business is included for reference. Teachers may choose to focus on this vocabulary through direct presentation, or may encourage the students to use this section for self-study.

## Grammar

There is no direct grammar instruction in the core lessons. However, a complete grammar resource has been provided at the end of the book. The grammar resource can serve as a reinforcement of the student's grammar skills. It can be used for self-study or independent practice or the teacher may choose to use material in class to present and practice language skills required by the productive exercises in the different lessons.

The language elements are ordered as they appear in the units. But they may be referred to in any order. Each grammar presentation provides a *grammar box* or paradigm followed by contextual examples and a practice exercise.

## Listening

Many of the workplace scenarios are presented and/or established through the listening contexts. Complete audio scripts and an audio CD have been provided for the student to allow for independent listening practice. Student access to audio scripts and CDs also provides multi-level instruction opportunities in the classroom.

## Ongoing Assessment

The five team projects found at the end of every unit, as well as the one-page unit reviews at the end of the book provide ample opportunity for ongoing assessment. Unit tests are provided in the Teacher's Resource Book.

# Unit 1

## Making your way

### Time to make a decision

**a** Read the following suggestions for finding a job and, in pairs, discuss which ones you agree with and why.

- ○ ▪ Contact your friends and see how they can help.
- ○ ▪ Visit an employment agency and ask about available jobs.
- ○ ▪ Look for the job that gives the best salary.
- ○ ▪ Read the advertisements in the Business Section of your local newspaper and try to find a job that matches your skills, qualifications, and interests.
- ○ ▪ Ask your parents or their colleagues to get you a job in the companies where they work.
- ○ ▪ Discuss your goals and interests with your friends and make a plan for how to proceed.
- ○ ▪ Talk to a counselor at the place where you are studying and ask for some advice.

**b** Listen to two friends talking about job hunting.
Check ✔ the points that are mentioned in their conversation.

CD T-1

_____ consult with different businesses and find out what is required in each department

_____ go to an employment agency

_____ look at some ads and see what is available

_____ think about your specific interest in business

_____ get in touch with any business contacts your family might have

_____ identify strengths and weaknesses for specific areas of business

_____ visit college counselor and discuss

**c** In pairs, practice making suggestions about how to start job hunting. Use the phrases in the box to help you.

| | |
|---|---|
| I think it's time to start . . . | We need to think about where . . . |
| Maybe we should begin by . . . | I suppose we should think about . . . |
| Let's go see . . . | We could find out about available jobs . . . |
| Why don't we read . . . | I suggest we start by . . . |

**d** Look at the following ads and underline the skills and qualifications needed for each job.

**1**

**Secretary/Receptionist**
required for Accountant firm in city center. Proficiency in MS Office, good interpersonal skills, and good telephone manners essential. Candidate should hold a diploma from a recognized business school. Experience an advantage though not a necessity. Apply with resume, copy of diploma and three references to . . .

**2**

**Accounts Manager**

Prestigious language school requires an Internal Accounts Manager to take responsibility for a number of key existing accounts together with the development of new business. Candidates, preferably graduates, with proven ability will report to the Director. Remuneration negotiable and based on qualifications and experience.

**3**

**Sales Representative** (rep) required for a small but dynamic automobile company. The selected candidate must enjoy all aspects of sales and be willing to research the latest car models. Ability to work in a team and a strong interest in the client are essential. No experience necessary as on-the-job training is provided. Basic salary and commission on car sales. Apply to . . .

**e** Read the ads again and answer the questions.

1. What qualifications are essential for the Secretary/Receptionist position?
_____

2. What responsibilities are listed for the Accounts Manager?
_____

3. From the new graduate's point of view, what advantages are offered by jobs 1 and 3?
_____

4. Is it essential that the Accounts Manager have a university qualification?
_____

5. What feature of the sales representative job might be a motivating factor?
_____

**f** Complete the following sentences with a suitable word used in any one of the three ads above.

1. Though we have stated what we are willing to pay a suitable candidate, the salary is in fact _____.

2. Experience and qualifications are _____ for this job and the candidate should have worked for at least three years with a reputable company.

3. One great _____ to this job is that there is an opportunity for on-the-job training.

4. No previous experience is _____ for the job of secretary as training is provided.

**g** In pairs, or small groups, discuss the relative merits of each of the three jobs.

## Lesson 2

# Following through

**a** In pairs, discuss these questions.

1. How many times have you had a telephone conversation in English?
2. What were the circumstances of the last English telephone conversation that you had?
3. What do you find especially difficult or easy about talking by telephone in English?

**b** Read and complete each space in the telephone conversation with the letter of the correct phrase from the box. The first one has been done for you.

> **a.** Is three o'clock okay for you?     **b.** Can I ask why you are calling?     **c.** See you on Thursday.
>
> **d.** May I ask who is calling, please?        **e.** When would you like to come in?

**Martha:** Good morning. Can I speak to Mrs. Mills, please?

**Personal Assistant:** (1) ___*d*___

**Martha:** My name is Martha Willis. I'm a student at the university.

**PA:** I'm afraid Mrs. Mills is in a meeting right now. (2) _____

**Martha:** I need some advice on finding a job. Can I make an appointment to see her?

**PA:** Yes. (3) _____

**Martha:** On Thursday afternoon if she is free.

**PA:** Let me check. Yes, that should be alright. (4) _____

**Martha:** Yes, it is.

**PA:** Fine. So, that's three o'clock on Thursday the 15th.

**Martha:** Yes. Thank you. Oh, and can you also include my friend John Jones?

**PA:** Yes, that's no problem. (5) _____

**Martha:** Thank you. Goodbye.

**PA:** Goodbye.

CD
T-2

**c** Listen to check your answers.

**d** Practice the complete conversation in pairs.

**e** The following words or phrases are commonly found on resumes. Categorize them in the chart below. Then add two more items in each section.

| high school diploma | theater and film |
| efficient | fluent in French |
| familiar with Microsoft Office | hard-working |
| swimming | B.A. |
| competent in conversational Spanish | independent |
| diploma in computer science | knowledge of the Internet |

| Personality | *precise, energetic* |
|---|---|
| Skills | *knows how to prepare business proposals* |
| Qualifications | *diploma in marketing* |
| Hobbies / Interests | *mountain biking, piano* |

CD
T-3

**f** Listen to Mrs. Mills' advice to Martha and John and complete the notes.

Looking for a job - various steps
match interests with skills, abilities,
personality.
Business - a very wide area: need
to think about
Human Resources: duties -
Sales and Marketing: - different
kind of challenge
focus -
Finance: be involved in

**g** Select a job in business that you think you would enjoy and, in your notebook, make a list of the qualifications, skills, and personality traits that you think are important for that job.

**h** In pairs, share and compare your opinions and give your reasons. Use the language in the chart to help you.

*In my opinion, a person who works in finance must be precise because making mistakes could cost a company a lot of money.*

| giving an opinion | I think, in my view, in my opinion, I believe |
| giving a reason | because, as, consequently, therefore, as a result |

# Filling out forms

**a** In pairs, combine verbs from box **A** with phrases from box **B** to form appropriate collocations. Some verbs and phrases may be used more than once.

*submit your application, follow instructions*

| A | make          proofread          short-list          submit          apply for |
|---|---|
|   | fill out          follow          leave          list |

| B | a section blank          the same steps          your abilities and skills |
|---|---|
|   | candidates          a job          the application form          your application |
|   | decisions          instructions          your most recent jobs |

**b** Read and complete the text with the correct words.

When you (1) ___apply___ for a job, you are usually asked to (2) _____ an application form as well as your resume and a cover letter. Companies like to have standardized forms containing information about candidates. This makes comparison simpler and also makes it easier for a company to (3) _____ candidates for interview. It is very important that you (4) _____ all your abilities and skills in the spaces provided.

Remember, this is an employer's first impression of you so it is very important that you (5) _____ the form accurately. Read the form very carefully and answer each question honestly and accurately. Show employers that you are able to (6) _____ instructions. Answer all questions as precisely and concisely as you can. Do not (7) _____ any sections blank. If a question does not (8) _____ to you, simply write "not applicable." Proofread your application before you turn it in.

**c** Complete the notes with key information from the text.

*why employers prefer to see job application forms:* _____

*how to fill out the form:* _____

**d** Read and complete the sentences with *up* or *in*.

1. A colleague called in sick today and so the manager asked me to fill _____ for him.
2. The lecture was boring and not very useful so he filled _____ the time sending text messages.
3. When Jane returned to work, I filled her _____ on what had happened while she had been away.
4. The conference room filled _____ very quickly, and at exactly ten o'clock, the CEO walked in.

**e** Now match the phrasal verbs from Exercise **d** with the correct meanings.

1. to fill in _____
2. to fill (someone) in _____
3. to fill up (no object) _____
4. to fill up (with object) _____

   a. to spend or use up (especially) surplus time
   b. to take someone's place temporarily
   c. to make or become completely full
   d. to supply someone with recent information

**f** Complete the sentences with the correct form of a phrasal verb with *fill*.

1. When my boss returns, I will have to _____ (him) on what happened while he was away.
2. John really wastes a lot of time. He _____ his day with useless online searches.
3. When you _____ an application form, don't leave any sections blank.
4. The restaurant was empty when we arrived, but it soon _____.
5. Rosa was going to take the day off, but she has to _____ for a sick co-worker.

**g** Look for more examples of phrasal verbs that have more than one meaning and make notes in your notebook.

**h** Listen to Martha and John talking about their strengths and weaknesses. Complete the following table with the information you hear.

CD
T-4

| | *Strengths* | *Weaknesses* |
|---|---|---|
| *John* | | |
| *Martha* | | |

 **i** In pairs, discuss what you see as your strengths and weaknesses and talk about how you could present any weaknesses in a more positive light.

## ■ Lesson 4

# Preparing your resume

**a** Read the following statements about preparing a resume and write whether you agree or disagree with each one. Then discuss your opinions in pairs.

When preparing a resume, you should . . .

(a) always give your age and marital status.          _____

(b) provide a current address and phone number.     _____

(c) always use your friends as references.           _____

(d) list all your employment experience.             _____

(e) always include copies of personal references.    _____

(f) use a reliable, non-gimmicky e-mail address.     _____

**b** Read the steps for preparing a resume and number them in the best order. The first one has been done for you. Then check your answers in pairs.

_____ Include a brief outline of your hobbies and interests.

_____ Provide the names of three references who can be contacted by a prospective employer.

__1__ Include your name, and current address, e-mail address, and telephone number(s).

_____ Outline your educational history starting with your most recent studies.

_____ Include other training and courses that you have taken.

_____ List your work experience starting with your most recent employment.

**c** Listen to a Human Resources manager talking about what to include in a resume. Check ✔ the items that should be included and mark with an ✘ those that should not.

CD
T-5

☐ address                    ☐ experience

☐ age                        ☐ interests

☐ all your education         ☐ marital status

☐ consenting references      ☐ religion

☐ e-mail                     ☐ volunteer work

**d** In pairs, take turns summarizing the advice offered in the previous exercise. Use expressions from the box or similar expressions to express obligation, recommendation, etc.

| | | | |
|---|---|---|---|
| You have to . . . | It is advisable to . . . | You shouldn't . . . | We advise you to . . . |
| Your resume should be . . . | Make sure you . . . | You should . . . | You do not have to . . . |

**e** Read this extract from an advertisement for a job at a large banking organization. Then read through the two resumes and decide which applicant is better suited to the job.

**Responsibilities:**
- Work as part of a team to take ownership of all HR functions within the bank including staff development, training, and all issues concerning staff welfare.
- Maintain all staff documents including contracts, leave, and sick benefits.
- Participate in internal and external recruitment procedures.

### Applicant 1

**Qualifications**

1982-84 Community College
Diploma in Business
On-the-job short courses in various aspects of HR and computer programs

**Experience**

1996-2006 Rights General Trading
Human Resources Manager
- Responsibility for all HR staff management
- Recruitment supervisor
- Adviser on all staff development issues

1984-96 RFC Food Co.
Human Resources Support Assistant
- Recruitment
- Employee contracts
- Organization of staff PD

### Applicant 2

**Qualifications**

2003-05 University of Birmingham
M.A. in Human Resources Management
2000-03 University of Cincinnati
B.A. Business Administration - special focus on Finance

**Experience**

2005-2006 More Mortgages Co.
Assistant in HR Department (temporary)
- Preparing documents and maintaining files on all applicants
- Sending letters of invitation to interview to short-listed applicants

2003-2005 Library Support
- Afternoon duties at circulation desk
- Organizing books on shelves

**f** Listen to two people from the Human Resources Department discussing the two **applicants**. Check ✔ the positive points for each applicant.

CD T-6

|  | *Applicant 1* | *Applicant 2* |
|---|---|---|
| *overall qualifications* |  |  |
| *specific courses* |  |  |
| *years of experience* |  |  |
| *range of responsibilities* |  |  |
| *experience related to finance* |  |  |
| *flexibility* |  |  |
| *team player* |  |  |

**g** Now, using the ideas and advice contained in this lesson, write your own resume.

## Lesson 5

# Sending it all off

**a** Read the statements and, in pairs, discuss business situations in which these statements would be appropriate or inappropriate.

1. "Hi, there. How're you doin' today?"
2. "Guys, we really need to stay in touch."
3. "It is important that managers communicate with each other."
4. "I've been feeling a bit under the weather recently."
5. "Great work, everybody! Keep it up!"
6. "We're facing tough competition, so we have to stay focused."

**b** Read the excerpts from two cover letters written by applicants for a job as a financial assistant. Consider the register of the excerpts and beside each one write *formal* or *informal*.

1. Anyway, you can send me an e-mail at the above address. Or call any time. _____

2. I enclose my resume and a completed application form. _____

3. I wish to apply for the position of Financial Assistant advertised recently (Ref. 23456). _____

4. Do you want me to send a resume? I haven't prepared one yet, but I guess it shouldn't take me too long. _____

5. So, can I come over and see you this week? You see, I'd like to get things together as soon as I can. _____

6. Since I graduated, I have been working with a small firm that arranges home loans. _____

7. To the position of Financial Assistant, I would bring up-to-date knowledge of computer programs used in financial analysis. _____

8. I received a diploma in finance a couple of years ago and right now I'm working for a friend's business._____

**c** In pairs, discuss your answers and make notes of the features of the informal excerpts that make them inappropriate for a cover letter.

**d** Read the sentences and think about the function of the underlined linking words. Below each sentence, write the correct language function from the box.

| | | | |
|---|---|---|---|
| show a time relationship | provide a reason | offer additional information | contrast two ideas |

1. I <u>also</u> enjoy working with people and I would bring energy and enthusiasm to the position.

   _____

2. <u>Since</u> I graduated, I have been working with a small firm that arranges home loans.

   _____

3. <u>Though</u> I am a recent graduate, I have already had some experience working in finance.

   _____

4. I have never worked for a large company and <u>so</u> this would provide a new challenge for me.

   _____

**e** Listen to a teacher talking to his students about e-mail etiquette. Read the sentences and check ✔ the correct box for each one.

CD
T-7

| | Do | Don't |
|---|---|---|
| 1. Write a business e-mail the same way you chat in a chat room. | ☐ | ☐ |
| 2. Omit the greeting at the start of a formal e-mail. | ☐ | ☐ |
| 3. Try to keep e-mails quite short. | ☐ | ☐ |
| 4. Include your name at the end of an e-mail. | ☐ | ☐ |
| 5. Compose an e-mail in one continuous paragraph. | ☐ | ☐ |
| 6. Let the computer take care of checking spelling. | ☐ | ☐ |
| 7. Feel free to include smiley faces on informal e-mails to friends. | ☐ | ☐ |

**f** You have just received the following e-mail. In your notebook, write an e-mail reply to Roger Davis confirming the date and time of your interview.

Adress: _____

Dear _____

I am pleased to inform you that you have been short-listed for an interview for the position of Financial Adviser at Morgan Finance. Your interview has been scheduled for Friday, April 13 at 1 p.m. Please confirm that this date and time are convenient for you. An e-mail reply will suffice.

Regards

**Roger Davis**

## ■ Lesson 6
# Finally it's time for the interview

**a** In pairs, discuss the questions.

1. When was the last time you attended an interview and what was it for?
2. How did you feel before, during, and after the interview?
3. How well (or otherwise) did the interview go?

**b** Combine the words or phrases in the box with either *make* or *do* and write phrases in your notebook.

> *do a computer course,*
> *make a decision*

| | | | | |
|---|---|---|---|---|
| progress | a course | a good impression | a job | a profit |
| an exercise | money | a favor | business | someone feel nervous |
| | your best | | your homework | |

**c** Complete the following sentences with a correct form of *make* or *do*.

1. Sarah realized she _____*had made*_____ a mistake when she saw her friend's face.
2. Tom _____ his best but he didn't get past the final interview.
3. There are so many good candidates for the job that it's hard _____ a decision.
4. Thank you very much. It has been a pleasure _____ business with you!
5. We are going to have to work very hard if we want _____ a profit.
6. Although Terry is a very good student, she hates _____ exams.

**d** Listen to some advice about interviews and check ✔ the appropriate boxes.

CD T-8

| | Do | Don't |
|---|:---:|:---:|
| 1. Observe the proper dress code. | ☐ | ☐ |
| 2. Wear bright and loud clothes. | ☐ | ☐ |
| 3. Show what you know about the company. | ☐ | ☐ |
| 4. Relax and just be yourself. | ☐ | ☐ |
| 5. Give a casual, informal greeting. | ☐ | ☐ |
| 6. Say negative things about past employers. | ☐ | ☐ |
| 7. Maintain good eye contact. | ☐ | ☐ |
| 8. Reply with short *yes* or *no* answers. | ☐ | ☐ |

**e** Complete the following interview with appropriate questions.

1. Q: _____
   A: I graduated from college in September 2005.

2. Q: _____
   A: Yes, I have had some work experience. I worked for four months with Brown and Co. in their Finance Department.

3. Q: _____
   A: I have heard a lot about your company and feel that I could learn a lot if I worked here.

4. Q: _____
   A: I enjoy working with people. In my last position, I worked on a project with four other young people and we shared the responsibilities well.

5. Q: _____
   A: I would like to gain some experience and then go on to do an MBA.

6. Q: _____
   A: I speak Spanish and a little French. I am also quite competent with Microsoft Office and I plan to take some special computer courses for finance.

7. Q: _____
   A: Well, I have been told that I am quite fussy about details, but I think it is very important to be accurate, especially in matters of accounting and finance.

**f** In pairs, discuss the interviewee's answers and make suggestions with regard to how, if at all, they could be improved.

**g** Having made any relevant changes, practice the interview in pairs.

**h** Listen to short excerpts from three interviews and then discuss the following questions in pairs or small groups.

CD
T-9

1. How well prepared is each interviewee for his/her interview?
2. How would you describe the emotional state of each interviewee?
3. What comments would you make about the quality of the interviewer's questions?
4. What comments would you make about the tone and formality of the interviews?

**i** Choose one of the interviewees who, in your opinion, did not perform well. In pairs, role-play a conversation in which you give that person some advice on how to handle interviews.

# Team Project 1

## Task:
### Prepare a recruitment dossier

You work in the careers advice center of a university. It is your job to advise students about career choices and to provide information about employment opportunities.

With your team:

1. Select a medium- to large-sized company in your town/city.

2. Consult the company's corporate website for general, background information.

3. Contact the Human Resources department of the company.

4. Ask for copies of any job advertisements that they have posted recently.

5. Ask for information about the process involved in hiring new employees.

6. Gather information on selection procedures and the short-listing of candidates.

7. Present your findings to the rest of the class.

# Unit 2

## Selling is what it's all about

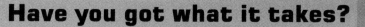

### Have you got what it takes?

**a** In pairs or small groups, discuss these statements.

1. Selling is about sticking your foot in the door and making a speech.
2. To be a good salesperson it helps if you like people.
3. It is essential to like what you are trying to sell.
4. Selling is always fun.
5. A salesperson needs to have a lot of initiative.

**b** In your notebook, make a list of the things that you think make a good salesperson. Then compare your ideas with a classmate's.

**c** Read the text and evaluate your personality in terms of the characteristics mentioned. Then compare and discuss your ideas in pairs.

## A suitable personality for the job

We are all a mixture of different characteristics. A person does not have just one type of personality or another, though people do show a tendency to be one way rather than the other. There are many ways to analyze personality. Here we will consider just four. The first, Type A personality tends to be highly driven and may be very competitive. Type As generally like to get recognition for their achievements, they can be very independent, and they may also be direct and to the point. They are likely to be very focused, persistent, and decisive.

While the Type B personality, like A, is quite extroverted, he or she is often much more sociable, and likes to party and have a good time even while working. Types C and D, on the other hand, have a tendency to be quieter and more introverted. Type C people usually pay great attention to detail, love accuracy, and are dependable and loyal, while Type D people generally enjoy guidelines and stick to deadlines

and schedules. In its own way, each personality type has characteristics that are valuable assets in a salesperson.

**d** Read the article again and find examples of the following types of expressions.

| expressions that show a tendency: | *tends to be, may be* |
|---|---|
| connectors that indicate contrast: | *while* |

**e** Use the following information to make sentences about each person's personality. Use expressions from Exercise **d**.

> Example:
> *Though Robert can sometimes be aggressive, at other times he can be very pleasant.*

Robert   aggressive at times / pleasant at other times
Chris    likes a good time while working / capable of achieving a lot
Naomi    generally very compassionate / very decisive and persistent
Mark     careless sometimes / usually accurate and precise

**f** Listen to a talk about what makes a good salesperson. Number the points in the order they are mentioned.

CD
T-10

1. be a good listener                                          _____
2. pick up on a person's personality traits                    ____1____
3. like people and recognize their needs and wants             _____
4. create an emotional link with the customer                  _____
5. sell products that you like                                 _____
6. recognize indecisiveness and help customers to make a decision  _____

**g** Look at these informal expressions from the first part of the talk and rewrite each one in more formal language.

1. sticking your foot in the front door     _____
2. bullying your way into a home             _____
3. conning the person                        _____
4. coughing up for a product                 _____

**h** Study the following phrasal verbs from the talk about salespeople. For each one, find a one-word verb with the same meaning.

1. turn out     _____
2. pick up on   _____
3. build on     _____
4. tune into    _____

**i** From what you have learned so far, write a short description of what makes a good salesperson.

## ■ Lesson 2

# How do you do it?

**a** In pairs, discuss the questions.

1. When was the last time you went shopping?
2. What did you buy and why did you buy it?
3. Have you ever bought something you had not planned to buy?
4. What was it that convinced you to buy on impulse?

**b** Beside each question, write the letter of the correct response from the box. Then, in pairs, discuss where you might hear these conversations taking place.

| | |
|---|---|
| a. I was looking for something around $250. | d. Usually a 6, but these look a little narrow. |
| b. I'm afraid we only have it in hardback. | e. Yes. It's an aid organization, isn't it? |
| c. Yes. In the next aisle, on your left. | f. Er . . . brown, please. |

1. Have you heard of Oxfam?                                  _____
2. What size do you take?                                        _____
3. Would you like brown or white bread?                  _____
4. Can you tell me where the organic produce is?     _____
5. How much were you thinking of paying?               _____
6. Do you have Marjorie Owen's latest novel in paperback? _____

**c** Role-play one of these situations in pairs.

| BUYING PERFUME | **Student A: Salesperson** Find out brand, size, amount of money willing to spend. | **Student B: Customer** Provide the information and make a decision on what you are offered. |
|---|---|---|
| BUYING A CAR | **Student A: Salesperson** Find out what the customer uses car for, model and year preferred, and budget. | **Student B: Customer** Provide the information and then decide that you need time to think it over. |
| BUYING A PAIR OF SHOES | **Student A: Salesperson** Find out the color, size, and type of shoe required. | **Student B: Customer** Take your time and ask to see many different pairs of shoes. |

**d** Complete the phrases or sentences with the verbs in the box.

| check | give | help | make | reduce | sign | speak | work |
|-------|------|------|------|--------|------|-------|------|

1. Can I _____ with Geraldine Murray, please?     _____*speak*_____
2. How can I _____ you?     _____
3. I _____ for Telefast, a cost-cutting company . . .     _____
4. . . . if there's a genuine way to help _____ my phone bills . . .     _____
5. Can you _____ me a quick explanation?     _____
6. We have a special offer if you _____ up this month.     _____
7. And if you _____ international calls at off-peak times . . .     _____
8. Can I just _____ that I have your correct address?     _____

**e** Identify the speaker of each sentence and write the numbers of the sentences in the chart.

| salesperson | *sentence #1* |
|-------------|---------------|
| prospective customer | |

**f** Listen to the telephone conversation to check your answers.

CD T-11

**g** Match each condition with the corresponding action.

| Condition | Action |
|-----------|--------|
| 1. If there's a way to help reduce my phone bills, . . . _____ | a. you need to apply right away |
| 2. If you are interested, . . . _____ | b. there is a 40% reduction |
| 3. If you make international calls at off-peak times, . . . _____ | c. count me in. |
| 4. If you want the free calls for a month, . . . _____ | d. just complete the application form and send it back |

**h** In your notebook, write conditional sentences using the following clauses.

1. you want to save money / check prices in different stores
2. you are happy with our offer / sign the contract and send it back
3. you require a demonstration of our products / salesman happy to do so
4. you shop online / save money
5. you want to contact someone quickly / send an e-mail

## Lesson 3

# Sales have increased by 20%

**a** Discuss the questions in pairs or small groups.

1. How often do you work with information presented in the form of bar charts or pie charts?
2. What sort of information is typically presented in this way?

**b** Study the bar chart and answer the questions.

1. What is the overall trend in organic food sales?
2. When did the greatest increase in sales occur?
3. What can you say about the sales figures between 2001 and 2003?

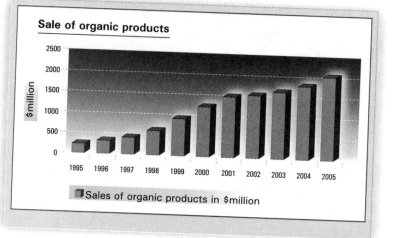

**c** Read this 2006 report about the growth of UK organic food sales and answer the questions.

Sales of organic food are booming, with demand sometimes outstripping supply. Sainsbury's, which attributes a large part of its continued recovery to this sector, has decided to boost supply by taking out long-term contracts with dairy farms while they convert to organic status. The supermarket's sales of organic milk have grown 74% in the last year, with the organic dairy market growing overall by 62.9%. Organic sales account for 4.4% of Sainsbury's total sales.

Other supermarkets have also reported dramatic increases in organic sales as consumers become more aware of health and more concerned about where their food comes from. Waitrose's organic food sales have increased by 20% in the year to January. It has a 17% share of the organic market but only 3.8% of the overall grocery market. Morrison's have seen their organic sales increase by 28% while Asda has reported growth in its organic sector of 12%, with a noticeable broadening of the socio-economic groups that now purchase organic food.

1. What is the significance for Sainsbury's of the increase in sales of organic food?
2. According to the report, why are more people buying organic food?
3. What is particularly notable about Waitrose's organic food sales?
4. What trend has been observed in the type of people who consume organic produce?

**d** Study these pairs of sentences. Then complete the table and add more examples of your own.

| adjective + noun |
| --- |
| There has been a **dramatic increase** in sales. |

| verb + adverb |
| --- |
| Sales have **increased dramatically**. |

| Adjective | Noun |
| --- | --- |
| slight | increase |
|  |  |
|  |  |
| noticeable | growth |
|  |  |

| Verb | Adverb |
| --- | --- |
|  |  |
| decrease | steadily |
| decline | sharply |
|  |  |
|  |  |

**e** In pairs, discuss **(a)** the benefits of using presentations in business, and **(b)** how you feel about giving presentations in front of an audience.

**f** Listen to the following advice about giving presentations and, for each point check ✔ the correct box.

|  | Do | Don't |
| --- | --- | --- |
| 1. Select essential information. | ☐ | ☐ |
| 2. Include all details. | ☐ | ☐ |
| 3. Come prepared with notes in order. | ☐ | ☐ |
| 4. Organize content in a logical way. | ☐ | ☐ |
| 5. Use the Introduction to inform listeners of contents. | ☐ | ☐ |
| 6. Include comments not related to the main topic. | ☐ | ☐ |
| 7. Establish a good relationship with audience. | ☐ | ☐ |
| 8. Avoid eye contact with audience. | ☐ | ☐ |
| 9. Speak quickly and loudly. | ☐ | ☐ |
| 10. Bring the talk to a proper conclusion. | ☐ | ☐ |

**g** Listen to three short presentations and evaluate each one according to the notes in the previous exercise. Add any extra comments of your own.

CD T-13

Presentation 1 _____

Presentation 2 _____

Presentation 3 _____

**h** Do some research into sales trends in a particular market in your country and prepare an oral presentation.

# Dealing with the customer

**a** Listen to a telephone call to a company that supplies furniture to large restaurants and hotels. Complete the notes about the order.

CD
T-14

| *Item* | *Quantity ordered* |
|--------|--------------------|
| double beds | |
| single beds | |
| closets | |
| dressers | |
| Order needed by: | |

**b** Listen to the conversation again and, in your notebook, make notes of the small talk between the two speakers before they get to the order.

CD
T-15

**c** In pairs, discuss whether or not it would be suitable to talk to a new customer about the following topics.

| | | |
|---|---|---|
| how the business is going | how the person's family is doing | the weather |
| how happy you are to take their order | | the customer's wife, husband, partner, etc. |
| | gossip about other businesses | |

**d** In pairs, role-play a telephone conversation based on the following situation. Use small talk where appropriate.

**Student A**
You work in the sales department of a wholesale outlet that sells bread and cookies.

**Student B**
You have just opened a small grocery store and you need to open an account with a supplier of bread and cookies.

**e** Listen to the telephone conversation between an employee at an organic food farm and a new customer and complete the order form.

CD
T-16

| Company | |
|---------|---|
| Delivery address | |
| Account number | |
| Purchase order # | |
| Order | |
| Transportation | |

**f** Read the customer complaints and use the prompts to write appropriate responses in the passive voice.

1. I placed an order for ten laptops three weeks ago.

   we / send out / the laptops / ten days ago

   *The laptops were sent out ten days ago.*

2. I placed an order for some new software last week.

   our staff / dispatch / your software / as we speak

   _____

3. I ordered three DVDs last Tuesday. When can I expect to receive them?

   we expect / those DVDs / today / we / should ship them to you / by Friday

   _____

**g** Using the notes on the right, write a short memo to a colleague asking him/her to track online an order that has not been delivered.

order requested: May 15th
sent out May 18th
Ref. number: RL 0098
85091
website:
www.maxcourier.com
inform me ASAP
Thanks

**h** Read and match each problem with a consumer expectation that is not being met.

**Problem**

1. You bought a 10-yard roll of cloth but later found that the last two yards were faded.
2. The person who came to install your central heating did not know how to do it.
3. Your new dining room table has a number of scratches on it.
4. A shirt sold to you as 100% silk in fact contains 50% polyester

**Rights of the consumer**

____ a. Goods should be in saleable condition without any faults.

____ b. Goods should match their description.

____ c. All pieces or parts of goods should be of the same quality as any sample.

____ d. Installation and service should be performed by qualified personnel.

**i** In pairs discuss occasions when your expectations as a consumer were not fulfilled.

## Lesson 5

# Dealing with complaints

**a** Do this experiment, in groups with three, five, or seven members.

1. What kinds of products or services do people often complain about?
2. Have you ever made a complaint about a product or service? How did you do it?
3. Have you ever wanted to make a complaint but did not? Why not?

**b** Listen to three customers who are seeking refunds. Take notes about each situation. Then, in pairs, discuss whether you think each customer should be given a refund.

CD
T-17

| Customer 1 | |
| --- | --- |
| Customer 2 | |
| Customer 3 | |

**c** Read the situations below. Then select two situations and role-play them in pairs. Take turns playing the parts of the customer and the store assistant. Use the expressions from the box to help you.

| | |
| --- | --- |
| I was wondering if I could exchange this . . . | I would like to return this . . . |
| Can I return this . . . ? | Is there anyone who could help me . . . ? |
| Do you think someone could take a look at this . . . ? | |

1. Mark bought a pair of running shoes in a store. After wearing them just three times, the sole of one shoe fell off. The store offered Mark a credit note for up to 80% of the value of the shoes.

2. Mrs. Jameson purchased a new microwave oven. After using it for three months, the timer broke. The store where she bought it denies responsibility and has suggested that she write to the manufacturer.

3. Amanda bought a pair of what she thought were fashionable shorts. Then she realized that that style was no longer in fashion. She tried to exchange the shorts but the store refused to give her a refund.

4. Nigel bought a sweater that the assistant said was 100% wool. Upon examining the sweater later he saw it was 50% wool, 40% polyester, and 10% nylon trim. The store says he is not entitled to a refund.

**d** In pairs or small groups, discuss the rights of the consumer in each of the cases.

**e** Listen to three dialogues between dissatisfied customers and salespeople. Take notes about the following points: the attitude of the customer and the salesperson, the resolution of the problem, your opinion of how each person handled the encounter.

CD
T-18

**f** Read the following letter and write the number of each item in the box next to the correct line of the text in the margin on the right.

| | | | |
|---|---|---|---|
| 1. desired outcome | 3. proof of purchase | 5. purpose of letter | 7. customer address |
| 2. signature | 4. salutation | 6. date | 8. problem |

10 Staines Avenue ☐
**Dartmouth, New Hampshire**

Tel: 9845321
**jerome@lycos.com**

April 3 ☐

Super Electrical Stores
6 Main Street
Dartmouth

Dear Sir/Madam, ☐

I am writing to you about a DVD player I purchased in your store on February 27. ☐ I enclose a copy of the receipt for $250. ☐

I managed to connect the DVD on March 1, but the sound was very poor. After a few days, it improved a little, but now a month after purchase there is no sound or picture from the machine. ☐

I am very disappointed with this purchase, especially since I have had excellent service from your store in the past. I would be grateful if you would replace this faulty DVD player with a new one as soon as possible. I can be contacted at the above address. ☐

Yours sincerely,

*Jerome Calvin*

**g** Write a reply to Jerome Calvin from Super Electrical Stores thanking him for his letter and his remarks about the company and apologizing for the problem. Explain that you are waiting for delivery of a new batch of electronic items and that as soon as they arrive you will replace the faulty one.

# Lesson 6

## Buying and selling on the Internet

**a** In pairs, discuss the questions.

1. Have you ever bought anything over the Internet?
2. What are the advantages and disadvantages of shopping online?

**b** Read the text and answer the questions.

M ike Gore, the founder of Booksandstuff.com, began his career as a software engineer. In the mid-1990s, he saw that Internet use was growing at a phenomenal rate each year. He saw in this a great business opportunity. He relocated to Seattle, where there was a large pool of technical know-how and, since the company began in 1996, it has generated billions of dollars in profits. Booksandstuff's customer base has grown to well over 30 million. The company has changed the way we do business.

So what are the secrets of Booksandstuff's success? First, the company is customer-centered, which means giving customers what they need. Customers don't have to travel to a bookstore—the store comes to them. Booksandstuff also aims to meet its customers' multi-product needs. The company has now expanded to include a broad range of products including music, videos, DVDs, toys, electronics, and household goods. Booksandstuff saves on storage space as it has a very quick turnaround. Payments are made immediately by credit card and items are shipped out in just a few days. One of Booksandstuff's distinctive features is its interactive and personalized service. Customers are invited to share their opinions about products and they can submit reviews of books and CDs. Customer information is stored and customers are alerted via e-mail about products similar to those that they have purchased before. Booksandstuff even helps customers create their own wish lists for gift giving.

1. Why did Mike Gore think that the Internet offered a great business opportunity?

_____

2. Why did Gore choose Seattle as his base?

_____

3. What is the key factor that has contributed to the success of Booksandstuff.com?

_____

4. How does Booksandstuff.com avoid spending a lot of money on storage space?

_____

**c** Find words in the text that mean the same as these words.

1. extraordinary (paragraph 1)   _____
2. produced (paragraph 1)   _____
3. extensive (paragraph 2)   _____
4. special (paragraph 2)   _____
5. notified (paragraph 2)   _____

**d** In your notebook, write complete sentences from these prompts with each verb in the correct tense.

1. Sophie / shop / online / for several years now
2. Daniel / work / Singapore / until 1999 / work in Japan / since then
3. online travel booking / change / the face / air travel
4. in the past / tourists / take / package holidays / independent travel / increase / recent years
5. Booksandstuff.com / not show / large profit / up to 2002 / since that year / profits / shoot up

**e** Listen to some advice about online shopping and complete the notes.

CD
T-19

> *Before you buy:* _____
>
> *How to pay:* _____
>
> *Precautions:* _____
>
> *Where to go for help:* _____

**f** Read the instructions for setting up an online store.
Number them in the correct order.

Selling things in an online store

____   Create a logo and upload it.
____   Prepare the appearance of your store—customize it.
____   Register your store in Internet directories.
____   Add categories for your items.
____   Receive payment and ship items.
____   Decide what to sell.

**g** Prepare a presentation in which you describe the procedure and discuss the pros and cons of this type of shopping with your classmates.

# Team Project 2

## Task:
### Prepare a consumer report

You work for a magazine that provides information about products and other issues relevant to consumers. It is your job to evaluate and compare products and prepare reports about them.

With your team:

1. Select the products that you want to compare.
2. Research and describe the features of your chosen products.
3. Describe the benefits of the products for the consumer.
4. Find out if it is possible to buy these products online.
5. Determine the cost of buying these products online as compared with a regular store.
6. Discuss the benefits of both types of shopping.
7. Present your findings to the rest of the class.

# Unit 3

# Marketing the product

**a** In pairs, discuss the questions.

1. Of the advertisements that you saw on your way here today, which caught your attention most?

2. What elements of an advertisement appeal to you—image? color? language? design? humor?

**b** Look at the following advertisements and write phrases from the ads in the appropriate categories.

ON SALE

**Quark Computer**

Lightweight, Faster processor
10% off

**14-in screen**
Regular price $1000
Today's SALE **Price** $900
1 yr. mfg. warranty

**STONY**

32-in High-Definition screen
4-speaker stereo sound system
3 yr. warranty
Regular price $900
**Today only** $810

THIS WEEK ONLY!

**All Sports Shoes Reduced**
(from 20% off)

*range of models*

In all TREADS models save an additional 15% off sales price.

| appearance | |
| --- | --- |
| choice | |
| durability | |
| after-sales service/protection | |
| feelings | |
| quality | *faster processor* |
| appealing features | |
| price/cost | |

**c** In pairs, answer these questions about the advertisements.

1. What products/services are these advertisements trying to sell?

2. What age group(s) and socioeconomic group(s) are they aimed at?

3. How effective do you find the advertisements?

**d** In pairs, discuss other advertisements that you have seen recently that caught your attention. Use expressions from the box to help you if you wish.

> This ad appeals to me because . . .      I find it attractive because of . . .
> I like the graphics and . . .     It gives me a sense of . . .     It makes me think of . . .

**e** Listen to a marketing expert explain about the different types of advertising. Complete the information in the notes.

CD
T-20

| Type of advertising | Type of information given | Type of product/service |
|---|---|---|
| Informative | | |
| Persuasive | | |
| Competitive | | |

**f** Complete the text with the verbs in parentheses in the present passive voice.

Advertising is an essential part of marketing a product and (1) _is used_ (use) to inform people about products and services. People (2)_____ (persuade) to buy products for different reasons. Sometimes they (3)_____ (convince) by the hope that the product will improve their appearance. Other times, they (4)_____ (make) to believe that a particular service is somehow better than any other. Often, a product (5)_____ (purchase) simply because it (6)_____ (need) in the home.

**g** In pairs, write an advertisement for a product or service. Decide on your target market and how to make your product sound attractive.

**h** Using the information in your advertisements, try to persuade classmates to buy your product or service. Use the language suggestions below.

| Persuasive language | Attractive sounding adjectives and phrases |
|---|---|
| You really must . . . <br> You really ought to . . . <br> You should try . . . | long-lasting / durable / tough <br> delicious / tasty / mouth-watering <br> safe / secure / guaranteed <br> cheap / inexpensive / unbeatable price <br> convenient / comfortable / simple to use |

## ■ Lesson 2

# Brands

**a** Discuss these questions in small groups.

1. Who in your group is wearing clothes or shoes of a well-known brand?
2. Why are these brands popular?
3. What is the difference between a *logo*, a *brand*, and a *trademark*? Think of examples of each.

**b** Look at the following words and symbols and answer the questions in pairs.

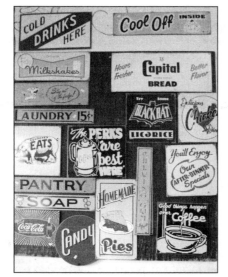

1. Which of these symbols do you recognize?
2. Are these words and symbols logos, brands, or trademarks?
3. What adjectives would you use to describe the products associated with these logos, brands, or trademarks?

**c** Listen to a talk on the development of branding over the years and check ✔ the statements that are true.

CD
T-21

1. Branding is a recent phenomenon. _____
2. One of the main functions of branding is to indicate ownership. _____
3. Branding in the past was similar to an artist's signature. _____
4. The function of all branding nowadays is to indicate social status. _____
5. Brands often have associations other than ownership _____
6. Brands nowadays are often associated with qualities a product is believed to have. _____
7. All brands today are seen as status symbols. _____

**d** Match the two halves of the sentences.

1. Brand names help customers identify . . .    __*d*__     a. distinguish one product from others.
2. A brand name ensures that we can . . .    _____    b. can make us feel comfortable.
3. Brand names that are familiar to us . . .    _____    c. have become status symbols.
4. The earliest types of brands helped . . .    _____    d. the manufacturer of a product.
5. Some of the best-known brands . . .    _____    e. to identify the maker of a product.

**e** Using a dictionary if necessary, write definitions in your notebook for the words and phrases in the box as they are used in the world of marketing.

| | | | |
|---|---|---|---|
| a market force | personalized service | innovative | revolutionary |
| market leader | | reliable | sophisticated |

**f** Complete each sentence with a word related to the word in parentheses.

1. A _____*revolution*_____ in research made the development of MP3 players possible.    (revolutionary)
2. Some car manufacturers have a reputation for safety and _____.    (reliable)
3. This car is well-known for its elegance and the _____ of its design.    (sophisticated)
4. _____ and research have kept this software company in the lead.    (innovative)

**g** Combine words from **Box A** with words from **Box B** to make compound adjectives.

**Examples:**

*mouth-watering, customer-friendly*

| A | mouth- | customer- | trouble- | energy- | well- |
|---|---|---|---|---|---|
| | cost- | family- | space- | user- | multi- | long- |

| B | known | purpose | size | cutting | free |
|---|---|---|---|---|---|
| | lasting | watering | friendly | saving | |

**h** Look at the chart of phrases for making comparisons. Add two more examples in each column of the chart.

| comparing things using short adjectives | comparing things using long adjectives | comparing things that are the same | comparing things that are not the same |
|---|---|---|---|
| X is cheaper than Y. | X is more popular than Y. | X is as good as Y. | X is not as reliable as Y. |
| | | | |
| | | | |

**i** In your notebook, write sentences comparing these pairs of items.

1. an economy car / a sports utility vehicle (an SUV)
2. home-cooked food / fast food
3. French perfumes / American perfumes

**j** Write a short description of a brand you are familiar with, pointing out its positive selling features and comparing it with other, similar products.

# Lesson 3
## Finding out what appeals to the consumer

**a** Discuss these questions in pairs or small groups.

1. When shopping, do you take notice of the design and layout of a store?
2. Do you like salespeople to help you or do you prefer to be left alone?
3. Do you think it is a good marketing strategy to give away free gifts?

**b** Take words from **Box A** and combine them with words from **Box B** to make appropriate collocations. With some words, more than one combination is possible.

| A | | | | | |
|---|---|---|---|---|---|
| | marketing | electronically | | latest | sales |
| business | special | | high | | customer-friendly |

| B | | | | | |
|---|---|---|---|---|---|
| offers | process | compatible | | designs | strategy |
| techniques | | sector | environment | standard | |

**c** Read the descriptions of these companies and label each one with the marketing strategy that they have adopted to keep their share of the market.

a. satisfying all the customer's needs in one store
b. speed of design and marketing
c. providing what the customer wants
d. compatibility of design and performance in all its products

1. This chain of luxury Caribbean hotels aims specifically at the mid- to higher-range segment of the tourist industry along with the business sector, and it aims to give customers exactly what they want.

2. This chain of electronics stores provides for all a person's needs in a customer-friendly environment. After customers make a purchase, the store offers them very attractive deals on other products. _____

3. This high-tech electronics company is world-famous and its products are highly valued. The design and technology of its products are of an extremely high standard and all of its electronic equipment are compatible. _____

4. This clothing retailer has a marketing strategy that is extremely successful—the speed with which it gets new clothes onto the shelves in the stores. It changes its stock regularly and customers flock in to catch the latest designs. _____

**d** Discuss these questions in pairs or small groups.

1. Have you ever answered questions for a market research survey in the street?
2. What sorts of products or services are researched using this method?
3. What sort of questions are people asked?

CD
T-22

**e** Listen to a talk about market research data collection techniques and check ✔ the correct column for each technique.

| Data collection technique | Primary | Secondary |
|---|---|---|
| Using questionnaires to find out people's likes and dislikes | _____ | _____ |
| Observing people as they shop in a store | _____ | _____ |
| Analyzing companies' sales reports | _____ | _____ |
| Conducting face-to-face interviews with consumers | _____ | _____ |
| Checking newspapers and government reports | _____ | _____ |
| Analyzing industry trade figures | _____ | _____ |
| Conducting consumer panels on TV and radio | _____ | _____ |
| Searching the Internet for data | _____ | _____ |

**f** You have been asked to conduct some market research about organic coffee. You must choose a data collection method from *direct mailing, telemarketing,* or *personal interviews.* Make notes about the advantages and disadvantages of each method. Take into account the factors listed in the box.

| | | |
|---|---|---|
| analysis time | how good the response rate is | cost of postage |
| how much time it takes up | telephone charges | preparation time |
| how wide an area can be covered | interviewers' fees | |

**g** Work in small groups. Compare and discuss your ideas and try to arrive at a consensus about one preferred data collection technique.

**h** Write some questions for a market research questionnaire to find out about consumers' opinions, attitudes, etc., about organic coffee or about another product of your choice.

**i** Compare and discuss your questions with those of a classmate.

# Lesson 4

## You too can do it—having a plan

**a** Look at the expressions in the box and, in pairs, discuss what you think they mean. Use a dictionary if necessary.

| ambush marketing | guerrilla marketing | viral marketing | blitz marketing |
|---|---|---|---|

**b** Read the text and complete each section with the correct heading from the box in **Exercise a**.

Just having a good product is not enough. You also need to market it well. Here are a few of the marketing strategies that companies have used in recent years.

1. _____: an entrepreneur starts small, produces a product or service that can outdo those of much larger companies, and spends nothing on advertising or promotion.

2. _____: a company attacks the targeted segment of the market with huge resources, advertising, and special offers.

3. _____: companies turn users of the Internet into unwitting (and unpaid) advertisers of their products.

4. _____: a company takes advantage of the presence of the media at an event in order to effectively advertise for free.

**c** Now listen to someone describing four companies. Match each example mentioned in the listening with a particular type of marketing strategy.

CD T-23

Company #1: _____
Company #2: _____
Company #3: _____
Company #4: _____

**d** Listen again. Find words in the listening that mean the same as these words and phrases.

CD T-24

| | |
|---|---|
| makes something easier | *facilitates* |
| introduction of a new product | _____ |
| persuading | _____ |
| expectation | _____ |
| completely covered | _____ |
| unwilling | _____ |
| approval | _____ |

**e** Complete the following sentences using either the present perfect or the past simple of the verb in parentheses.

1. He _____ (design) some new graphics software over the last few months.
2. Steve _____ (start) the company three years ago and it _____ (grow) at a remarkable pace since.
3. Since online stock brokering _____ (begin) in 1997, the practice _____ (increase).
4. I hope everybody _____ (receive) a copy of the agenda for the meeting.
5. Since the birth of the World Wide Web in the early 1990s, Internet use _____ (expand) at an incredible rate.

**f** Discuss your answers in pairs and decide if there are sentences where either the present perfect or the past simple tense could be used.

**g** Lisa's boss has asked her to e-mail all staff and inform them of the meeting scheduled for 3 p.m. on Wednesday, April 26. Read her e-mail and then discuss the questions in pairs.

1. What information has Lisa forgotten to include?
2. Is the tone and the language of her message appropriate? Why or why not?

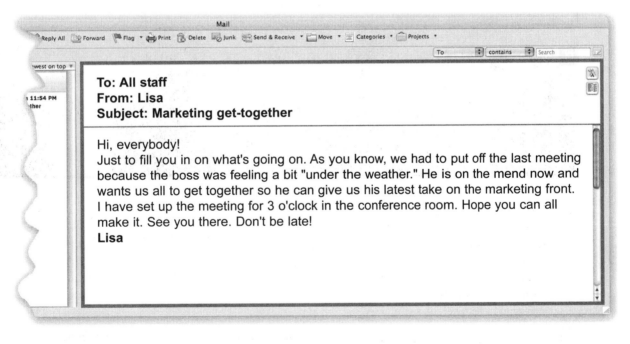

Mail

Reply All   Forward   Flag ▾   Print   Delete   Junk   Send & Receive ▾   Move ▾   Categories ▾   Projects ▾

To ▾ | contains ▾ | Search

west on top ▾

11:54 PM
ther

**To: All staff**
**From: Lisa**
**Subject: Marketing get-together**

Hi, everybody!
Just to fill you in on what's going on. As you know, we had to put off the last meeting because the boss was feeling a bit "under the weather." He is on the mend now and wants us all to get together so he can give us his latest take on the marketing front. I have set up the meeting for 3 o'clock in the conference room. Hope you can all make it. See you there. Don't be late!
**Lisa**

**h** Rewrite Lisa's e-mail in your notebook using the words and phrases in the box or other suitable expressions of your choosing. Delete any material that you think is inappropriate.

| inform you | recent developments | postpone | not feeling well | recovered |
|---|---|---|---|---|
| meet | bring us up to date | arranged | expect to see you there | |

## Lesson 5
# Getting together and understanding it all

**a** In pairs, make a list of some reasons why meetings are held.

**b** Listen to two employees discussing an upcoming meeting and complete the notes on the reasons given why meetings are important.

CD
T-25

|  |  |
|---|---|
| _____ *talk things over* | face to face |
| clear up _____ |  |
| _____ | new proposals and |
| developments |  |
| _____ | decision-making |
| opportunities to give _____ | _____ |
| involved in planning and __ | _____ our ideas |

**c** In pairs, discuss the meanings of these words from the listening.

| ambiguous | to be briefed | to input |
|---|---|---|

**d** Skim the text quickly and complete each paragraph with one of the following headings:
*Growth*    *Decline*    *Maturity*    *Development*

### The Marketing Life Cycle of a Product

1. _____ Products are developed and brought to the marketplace because of an established demand. However, during this first phase, the market is generally not fully developed, and sales—and growth in sales—may be slow at this initial stage.

2. _____ As a product becomes more established, demand expands and accelerates and the product's market share broadens. Sales increase rapidly and this stage is known as "take-off" stage.

3. _____ As time passes, demand gradually levels off and growth ceases. Purchasing of the product is generally the result of replacement demand rather than new growth.

4. _____ In the final marketing phases, the product loses its appeal for the consumer possibly because of competition from a new product. Sales go into a downward spiral and the product may even be taken off the market.

**e** Read the text again more carefully and write in your notebook brief definitions of the following words or phrases.

| loses appeal | levels off | ceases | downward spiral | take-off stage |
|---|---|---|---|---|

**f** Listen to the conversation and answer the questions.

CD T-26

1. What topic is being discussed?

2. What is the professional relationship between the two people?

**g** Listen to the conversation again and number these points in the correct order.

CD T-27

_____ Sales forecasts and targets

_____ Organizing marketing research—preparation of questionnaires

_____ Budget arrangements for product

_____ Any matters arising out of minutes

_1_ Read the minutes of the last meeting

_____ Any other business

_____ Welcome new staff members

_____ Planned timeframe for research and analysis

_____ Apologies for absences

**h** In pairs, discuss these questions about the conversation.

1. What language is used to ask someone to do something?

2. What is the general tone of the conversation?

3. What other expressions do you know for making requests

**i** In pairs, role-play one of the following situations.

**Student A:**
You are Mr. Steiner. Ask Tom (Student B) to organize the market research questionnaire and ask when it will be ready.

**Student B:**
You are Tom. Ask Mr. Steiner (Student A) for more information about the market research questionnaire.

**Student A:**
You are Mr. Steiner. Ask Lisa (Student B) to organize another meeting for the sales managers.

**Student B:**
You are Lisa. Ask Mr. Steiner (Student A) for details of the time and place for the meeting.

**Student A:**
You are Tom. Ask Lisa (Student B) to find some useful websites about market research.

**Student B:**
You are Lisa. Ask Tom (Student A) how soon he needs the information as you are very busy.

# Lesson 6

# If you can make it, they can fake it

 **a** Discuss these questions in pairs or small groups.

1. How often do you see pirated imitations of well-known brands for sale in your country?

2. Have you ever bought something that you knew was an illegal copy?

**b** Look at the words and phrases in the box and, for the moment, just check ✔ the ones that you know the meaning of.

| | | | |
|---|---|---|---|
| intellectual property rights | counterfeit | fake | to sue |
| a tip-off | to clamp down on | electronically tagged | to track down |
| global merchandise trade | to crack down | to confiscate | |

 CD T-28 **c** Listen to the first part of a talk on counterfeiting and fake goods and complete the notes.

*Problem: counterfeiting is a violation of*

*% of global merchandise that is pirated:*

*Annual loss in trade in dollars:*

*% of medicines that are counterfeit:*

CD T-29 **d** Listen to the next part of the talk and match the countries with the pirated goods.

1. USA _____     a. car windshields

2. Brazil _____     b. pharmaceuticals, cigarettes, $100 bills

3. China _____     c. parts for cell phones

4. Guam _____     d. pills for controlling cholesterol

5. France _____     e. printer cartridges

CD T-30 **e** Listen to the last part of the talk and answer these questions in pairs.

1. Which country represents the biggest problem in terms of violations of property rights?

2. Why is the Chinese government now starting to clamp down more on illegal copying?

3. What are multinational companies doing to fight the problem of illegal counterfeiting?

**f** Now check again the meaning of the words and phrases in **Exercise b**.

**g** In each sentence, replace the underlined multiword verb with the correct form of a word or phrase from the box.

| discover | find | increase | result in | produce | control | hear | account for |
|----------|------|----------|-----------|---------|---------|------|-------------|

1. Illegal copying of all kinds of goods really <u>took off</u> in the 1990s.  _____*increased*_____
2. Counterfeiting now <u>makes up</u> about 5 to 7% of world trade.  _____
3. Counterfeiting <u>gives rise to</u> $512 billion lost income annually.  _____
4. Police <u>picked up</u> information.  _____
5. Authorities <u>came across</u> a store of counterfeit Buick windshields.  _____
6. Two-thirds of fake goods are <u>turned out</u> in China.  _____
7. The Chinese government is beginning to <u>clamp down</u>.  _____
8. Detectives are trying to <u>track down</u> counterfeit companies.  _____

**h** Match the two parts of the sentences.

1. Pirated goods often closely resemble the originals . . .  ___*d*___
2. Brand-name goods are fashionable but very expensive . . .  _____
3. Since pirated goods are often much cheaper than the originals, . . .  _____
4. Because famous brand-name goods are symbols of luxury and status, . . .  _____
5. Since for many women the handbag is an important accessory, . . .  _____
6. Companies sometimes dump unassembled product components . . .  _____
7. Due to the fact that many customs officials are not qualified to deal with counterfeiters, . . .  _____

a. representatives from brands are called in when a fake is suspected.
b. those are the ones that are most frequently copied.
c. and this results in components being combined with inferior parts and sold as genuine articles.
d. and so it is difficult to identify the fakes.
e. there is a huge demand for affordable fake handbags.
f. consumers save money by buying the fake goods.
g. and consequently, these goods are copied and sold at a cheaper price.

**i** In your notebook, write more sentences about the problem with pirated goods. Show cause-and-effect relationships using connecting phrases like *owing to, because, due to, consequently,* etc.

## Task:
### Prepare a report about a franchise opportunity

You and your friends are interested in setting up your own business by buying the right to use the brand name of a well-known company.

With your team:

1. Choose a business that interests you.

2. Find as much general information as you can about franchising and, in particular, about the brand that you are interested in.

3. Establish what you need to set up the business.

4. Find out what the franchiser actually offers.

5. Establish the cost of setting up the franchise.

6. Present your findings to the class.

# Unit 4

## Financial matters

**a** In pairs or small groups, brainstorm a list of the expenses that students have to pay when they are away at college.

*Expenses*

**b** Listen to two students talking about the expenses they expect to have as they start out on their own. Complete the chart.

CD T-31

|  | Tuition |  | Utilities |  |  |  | Transport | Recreation |
|---|---|---|---|---|---|---|---|---|
| Michelle | 500 | 400 |  |  | 300 | 0 |  |  |
| Roger |  |  | 50 | 70 |  | 0 |  |  |

**c** Anne is planning to do an MBA and she is calculating her income and expenses for the coming year. In pairs, estimate what you think her income might be and complete Column A in the chart. Use some of the phrases in the box to help you.

| I think she probably earns . . . | It is possible that she . . . | It is likely that she . . . |

| Annual Income | A | B |
|---|---|---|
| Saved earnings from summer job | | |
| Part-time work during coming year | | |
| Savings | | |
| Grants | | |
| Other income | | |
| Total income for academic year | | |

**d** Now listen and complete **Column B** of the chart. Then compare and discuss your estimates with your classmates.

CD T-32

**e** Now listen and make notes of Anne's projected expenses.

CD
T-33

---

*Monthly Expenses*

| | |
|---|---|
| Rent | 400 |
| Books / School supplies | _____ |
| Food / Household supplies | _____ |
| New clothes | _____ |
| Entertainment | _____ |
| Telephone | _____ |
| Transportation | _____ |
| | _____ |
| Total *monthly* expenses | _____ |
| x 10 = Total *annual* expenses | _____ |

---

**f** In pairs, discuss the following questions.

1. Which of Anne's expenses are fixed?

2. Which of her expenses are variable?

3. Why won't Anne rent a place of her own this year?

4. Why does Anne expect her expenditure on transportation to be low?

5. Which expense does Anne intend to eliminate completely?

6. What do you think of Anne's decision to ask for a bank loan of $5,000?

**g** In small groups, role-play conversations about your expected expenditure on various items.

**Examples:**

How much do you think you'll have to spend on rent every month?

What do you think your transportation expenses will be each month?

**h** Write a paragraph about your thoughts regarding expenditure for a year's study away from home. Use the expressions in the box to help you.

| | | | |
|---|---|---|---|
| I need to figure out . . . | I should plan . . . | I'll probably need . . . | I'll have to stay . . . |
| | I may need to borrow . . . | I'll definitely have to cut down on . . . | |

 **i** Compare and discuss your ideas in pairs.

**a** Discuss these questions in pairs.

1. What advantages are there in opening a bank account?

2. What would a bank gain from having you as a customer?

**b** Look at the brochure and answer the questions.

1. What sort of a brochure is this?

2. Have you ever come across similar material? Where?

3. Who is it designed for? Why do you think so?

**Student Account**

This is an offer with mutual benefits—in other words, it's good for you and it's good for us. There's a good chance that in five to ten years' time, you could be a successful entrepreneur running your own business. By then, as one of our best clients, your good reputation will be your collateral in securing loans. Therefore, we want to invite you to join us now with this great special offer.

*What's in it for me?*
- a bank card that lets you withdraw money at thousands of ATMs nationwide
- free advice and counseling about saving and money management
- free bonus credit for your mobile phone if you pay with your bank card
- no bank charges—we don't charge you for having an account with us
- free monthly statements so that you can check your balance and keep track of your income and expenses
- discount card that gets you a 10% discount at selected music and sports stores

*So what do I have to do?*

It couldn't be easier! Stop by your local branch. Just bring a current ID—a passport or a driver's license is fine—and a recent bill (utilities, telephone, etc.) with your name or your parent's name and address on it.

**c** Read the text and answer the questions.

1. In your opinion, which of the benefits offered by the bank are of greatest value to students?

2. What advantages are there for banks in making special offers to students?

3. Why might students in particular need advice on money management?

4. Why would it be advantageous for music and sports shops to offer a discount?

**d** Using a dictionary if necessary, write definitions of these words as they are used in the text.

1. mutual _____

2. entrepreneur _____

3. collateral _____

4. withdraw _____

5. charges _____

6. balance _____

 **e** In pairs or small groups, discuss the style and tone of the brochure in **Excercise b**. Focus in particular on the words, expressions, contractions, etc., that give the text an informal feel.

**f** Chris is a student who wants to apply for a credit card. Listen to his conversation with a bank employee and complete these notes.

CD
T-34

> Why Chris needs a credit card:
> Application procedure:
> Repayment options:
>     1.
>     2.
>     3.
> Bank employee's recommendation:
> Annual charges:
> Interest rate:

**g** You have received the following letter from your bank about an overdue payment on your credit card. You recently moved and did not receive the first notice of payment. In your notebook, write a letter to the bank apologizing and explaining what happened. Mention that you include a check for the total amount owed.

Dear Ms. / Mr. _____,

    Our records indicate that you have not paid the minimum amount outstanding on your credit card. This money is now three weeks overdue. We regret to inform you that we are forced to suspend your credit card until full payment is made. As soon as payment is made, credit card facilities will be restored.

Sincerely,
Greg Richards, Student Accounts Manager

## Lesson 3

# Managing expenses

**a** In pairs or small groups, answer the questions.

1. What do you know about the financial and accounting side of business?
2. Would you like to work in the financial and accounting department of a company? Why or why not?

**b** In pairs, match each word or phrase in the box with the correct definition.

| capital | liabilities | balance sheet | fixed assets |
|---|---|---|---|
| debtor | current assets | creditor | inflation |

1. a person, group, or organization that owes money _____
2. assets that a business has and uses over a long period of time _____
3. a person, group, or organization to whom money is owed _____
4. the rate of increase in the price of goods over a period of time _____
5. accumulated wealth especially money used to produce more wealth _____
6. a statement showing the financial position of a business _____
7. assets that can change from day to day _____
8. current and fixed debts and expenses that must be paid _____

**c** Listen to this Finance Director and complete the balance sheet with the correct numbers.

CD
T-35

```
Fixed Assets:
            Buildings           400,000
            Equipment           _____
            Motor Vehicles      _____
------------------------------------------
            Total               510,000

Current Assets:
            Stock               _____
            Cash                2,000
            Trade debtor        _____
------------------------------------------
            Total               14,000

Current
Liabilities:
            Bank overdraft      _____
            Trade creditors     800
------------------------------------------
            Total               3,300
```

**d** Now use the information in the balance sheet to complete these calculations.

1. **Working capital** (current assets - current liabilities) = _____
2. **Total net assets** (fixed assets + working capital) = _____

**e** Read the article and decide if the statements are *true* or *false*.

# Itsbuzzin.com

Itsbuzzin.com was created in 1998 to sell fashion clothing over the Internet. By the time the company was liquidated in May 2000, huge amounts of capital had been spent on the venture. The Financial Times described Itsbuzzin.com as "Europe's first big Internet casualty."

What went wrong? Company founders spent $120 million on start-up and within a few months the company was valued at $380 million. However, bad management decisions led to spiraling costs that brought the company down. Its expected success was based on predictions that online shopping would increase to $20 billion by 2005. Online shopping has increased, but the market analysis for clothing products was not accurate.

But this was not the only problem. The overall financial outlay of Itsbuzzin.com was too high. Huge investments were made in complex website technology, which then experienced problems that drove costs even higher. The online catalog was very expensive—it had to be translated into several European languages—and it then needed further expenditure to keep it updated. Large numbers of staff were hired, resulting in a huge payroll and enormous expense accounts. The company offered free delivery, which created very high postal costs. When items were returned, delivery costs doubled. Itsbuzzin.com found itself in serious trouble and eventually collapsed. Major shareholders lost vast sums of money, advertising agencies were owed around $25 million, and many staff members went unpaid.

| | | |
|---|---|---|
| 1. The Itsbuzzin company started up with $380 million. | True | False |
| 2. Market analysis for online fashionwear sales was not realistic. | True | False |
| 3. Itsbuzzin's high operating costs were one of the major causes of its failure. | True | False |
| 4. Advertisers, shareholders, and staff were compensated for their losses. | True | False |
| 5. Staff spoke different languages and so there were large expense accounts. | True | False |
| 6. Offering free delivery turned out to be a very expensive decision. | True | False |

**f** In pairs, discuss the meaning of these words and phrases from the text. Then write a definition for each term in your notebook

| | | | |
|---|---|---|---|
| liquidated | venture | casualty | spiraling costs |
| financial outlay | payroll | expense accounts | shareholders |

**g** In pairs or small groups, discuss these questions.

1. What lessons can be learned from the experience of Itsbuzzin.com?

2. If you were in charge of a company, how would you try to reduce expenses and save money?

3. Do you know of any other online businesses that failed? What went wrong?

## Lesson 4

# Economic issues

**a** In pairs, discuss these questions.

1. What is inflation?
2. What are some of the causes of inflation?
3. Which countries currently have a high level of inflation?
4. What is the current level of inflation in your country?

**b** Match the two halves of the sentences.

1. Inflation can be defined as . . . _____
2. One factor that can result in inflation is . . . _____
3. Average inflation in the USA has been steady . . . _____
4. When interest rates go up and the cost of borrowing increases, . . . _____
5. Most people are able to cope with the average inflation rate of 3% . . . _____

a. as they get an annual increase in wages.
b. an increase in government taxes and fees.
c. a substantial and continuing overall increase in the general level of prices.
d. at about 3% a year for the last thirty years.
e. the cost of running a business increases and inflation can result.

**c** Listen and complete the chart with the correct prices for February and March.

CD
T-36

| Item | February | March | Inflation | April |
|------|----------|-------|-----------|-------|
| milk (1 liter) | $1.50 | | | |
| yogurt (500g) | | | 0% | |
| loaf of bread | | $3.05 | | |
| sugar (1 kilo) | $2.00 | | | |
| apples (1 kilo) | | | 5% | |
| teabags (100) | $2.20 | | | |
| coffee (500g) | | | -12.5% | |

**d** Now calculate the rate of inflation on each item as a percentage. Then work in pairs making predictions about the cost of each item in the chart for the month of April.

**e** Read and complete the interview with the appropriate questions.

1. Q: _____ *Who makes decisions in a free enterprise system?* _____

   A: Decisions in a free enterprise system are made by individuals.

2. Q: _____

   A: They can decide on the goods they want to produce and how their business should be run.

3. Q: _____

   A: In a centrally planned economic system, the government decides, for example, what goods and services can be produced and where businesses can be located.

4. Q: _____

   A: China is an example of a centrally planned economic system.

5. Q: _____

   A: A mixed economy is a system that is a combination of free enterprise and centrally planned systems.

6. Q: _____

   A: Decisions are made both by businesses and by the government. Businesses are free to plan and produce but there is also government intervention in certain matters.

**f** In pairs or small groups, discuss these questions.

1. What sort of economic system operates in your country?
2. What effects does this economic system have on the way businesses are run?

**g** Look at this chart, which contains information about commodities that the UK both imports and exports. In groups, discuss your reactions to the information in the chart.

| Commodity | Imports (tons) | Exports (tons) |
|---|---|---|
| cocoa / chocolate | 391,432 | 170,652 |
| fresh apples | 469,466 | 18,568 |
| sugar | 1.58 million | 767,225 |
| office machines | 172,285 | 82,067 |
| lumber | 4.83 million | 182,054 |
| fish | 626,032 | 386,055 |
| cement | 1.62 million | 480,357 |

**h** Look for information about commodities that your country both imports and exports and prepare a written report.

# Investments

**a** Look at the photograph and discuss the questions in pairs.

1. Where was this photograph taken?
2. What is going on in the photograph?
3. Where are stocks and shares traded in your country?
4. Where is information about stock markets published?

**b** Complete each sentence with one of the words or phrases from the box.

| | | | | | |
|---|---|---|---|---|---|
| stock | stock market | volatility | volatile | fraud | fraudulent |
| diversified portfolio | portfolio | liquidity | liquid | hedge | hedging |

1. He advised me to buy some _____ in a successful software company.
2. You should maintain a _____ in case there's a sudden change in the market.
3. They have paid out a lot in cash recently there by creating some _____ problems.
4. The _____ of some exchange rates makes it hard to predict what will happen.
5. The financial director is on trial for _____ arising from illegal insider dealing.
6. He keeps some low-risk savings income as a _____ against market volatility.

**c** Listen to a conversation about various types of investments and complete the chart with the appropriate information.

CD
T-37

| Investment type | Advantages | Disadvantages |
|---|---|---|
| stocks and shares | | can lose all your money including the principal |
| bonds | guaranteed the return of your money along with promised interest payments —no risk | |
| fixed-interest investments | | returns are low / investment generally tied in for a fixed time period |
| property | high returns possible relatively safe—property holds value, can borrow against value of property | |
| index futures | | need to be well informed depends on ability to predict direction of demand |

**d** Look at the graph and, in your notebook, write a short summary of the information that it shows.

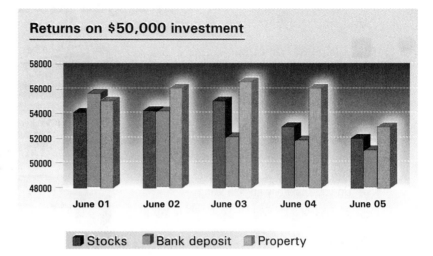

**Returns on $50,000 investment**

☐ Stocks   ☐ Bank deposit   ☐ Property

**e** In pairs, discuss which of the three options shown in the graph turned out to be the best investment. Give your reasons.

**f** Unscramble these sentences and rewrite each one in the correct order.

1. fell last year / from / as competition / Profits / hit / futures trading / commissions

   *Profits from futures trading fell last year as competition hit commissions.*

2. oil production / Astral Energy's / of Star Oil / boosted / acquisition / by 32%

   _____

3. by / Asset management / 21% / made strong progress / to 12 million / with profits up / of the firm

   _____

4. selling strongly / turned in / Whizz / books / a good performance / with Rowe's / in the first quarter

   _____

5. to register / of $8 million / out of the red / last year, / a loss / After lifting itself / BGH slipped back

   _____

6. through the wringer / due to / Shareholders / volatile behavior / have been put / the market's

   _____

**g** In pairs, discuss the meaning of these phrases taken from the sentences.

| the first quarter | to be in the red | acquisition | put through the wringer | futures trading |
|---|---|---|---|---|

**h** In your notebook, write definitions of these terms that could be understood by a layperson.

## Lesson 6

# Changes in the way we do things

**a** In pairs, discuss the questions.

1. What is the difference between *jargon* and *slang*?
2. How much English jargon do you know and use in your particular field of work or study?
3. Do you know any English slang expressions related to your field of work or study?

**b** Match the letter of each investment term with the correct definition.

| a. baby bond | b. bear market | c. correction | d. daisy chaining | e. dead cat bounce |
|---|---|---|---|---|
| f. bull market | g. boom | h. sleeper | i. wallflower | j. widow-and-orphan |

1. ___d___ the illegal practice of creating artificial transactions to give the appearance of activity and interest in a particular stock
2. _____ a very safe stock in a non-cyclical industry, usually paying large dividends
3. _____ a prolonged period in which investment prices rise faster than their historical average
4. _____ a quick, moderate rise in the price of a stock following a precipitous decline
5. _____ a stock that has been largely ignored by research analysts, because it is small or in an out-of-favor sector
6. _____ a stock that is trading at an unusually low valuation based on traditional measures
7. _____ a prolonged period in which investment prices fall, accompanied by general pessimism
8. _____ a bond that has a par value less than $1,000
9. _____ a period of rapid economic expansion
10. _____ a reversal of the prevailing trend in price movement for a security, most often a decline after a period of rising prices

**c** Listen to a talk about online investment trading and complete the notes with the relevant information.

CD T-38

*Online trading*

*first essential step:*

*comparative studies:*

*instant placement:*

*how much to invest:*

**d** In pairs, discuss the meaning of these words and phrases from the listening material.

| maximize your profits | do your homework | trustworthy | bear in mind | placement |
|---|---|---|---|---|

**e** Discuss these questions in pairs or in small groups.

1. What financial transactions can be carried out online nowadays?
2. Which of these transactions have you tried? How was it?

**f** Read and complete this interview about online banking.

1. Q: _I want to do my banking online. What do I need?_
A: All you need for 24/7 online banking is an Internet connection.
2. _____
A: Yes, you can. All your household bills can be paid online.
3. _____
A: Certainly. You can schedule automatic direct debit to pay your regular bills.
4. _____
A: You can view your account whenever you want. Your bank issues you with a special PIN.
5. _____
A: Copies of all your transactions can be printed out and kept for your records.
6. _____
A: If you need a loan, you can research what is available and make an online application.
7. _____
A: You can transfer funds to anyone via electronic bank transfer.
8. _____
A: Most banks offer a 24-hour customer support service to deal with problems.
9. _____
A: You can register online. You could do it right now!

**g** In pairs, compare and discuss your questions. Then use the information in the interview to role-play a conversation about online banking.

**h** Research and prepare a written report about either a) online trading in stocks or b) online banking services.

## Task:
**Prepare a report about retail credit services**

You have been asked to prepare a report for a consumer magazine on the subject of retail credit cards.

With your team:

1. Choose two of three large department stores that operate in your town/city.

2. Find out as much as you can about how their credit cards operate.

3. If possible, make appointments to speak with people from the relevant finance and credit departments.

4. Find out about the risks involved in doing business in this way.

5. Find out what abuses of the credit system can occur and what sort of losses can be incurred.

6. Find out about any insurance and protection measures that have been implemented.

7. Present your findings to the rest of the class.

# Unit 5

# Global concerns

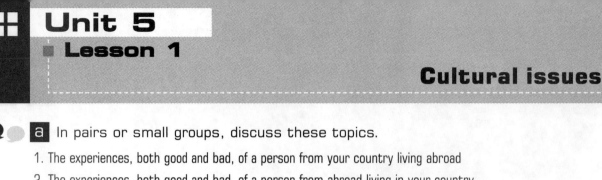

**a** In pairs or small groups, discuss these topics.

1. The experiences, both good and bad, of a person from your country living abroad

2. The experiences, both good and bad, of a person from abroad living in your country

**b** Complete the flow chart with words from the box.

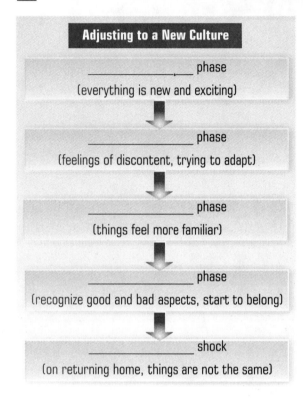

**Adjusting to a New Culture**

_____ phase
(everything is new and exciting)

_____ phase
(feelings of discontent, trying to adapt)

_____ phase
(things feel more familiar)

_____ phase
(recognize good and bad aspects, start to belong)

_____ shock
(on returning home, things are not the same)

| | |
|---|---|
| Integration | Understanding |
| "Honeymoon" | Re-entry |
| Transition | |

**c** Read these comments from people who are living in another country. From each person's description, discuss in pairs what stage you think that person is at according to the flow chart above.

*"I'm beginning to feel more comfortable here and I think I'm beginning to tune in to the sense of humor. It is definitely different from Chinese humor, but I am starting to catch on."* Sophie

"It's so great to be here! I can't wait to get out and explore and get in on the action here. Everything is so fascinating!" Marcus

"I feel so at home here now that if I went back to Japan I'm sure I would feel out of place there. It's strange isn't it how things turn out? I was so lonely when I first arrived." Yukiko

"It's just like anywhere else—some things go well, some go badly. Once you work out how the system works, you can get on with things more easily."

Antonio

"I'm so fed up with this place! The weather is terrible—all this wind and rain. I hate it and I really want to go home!" Luciana

**d** Match each phrasal verb from the previous exercise with the correct meaning below.

1. tune in     _b_     a. happen in the end
2. catch on    _____    b. be aware of
3. get in on    _____    c. continue
4. turn out    _____    d. discover, solve
5. work out    _____    e. take part in
6. get on    _____    f. understand

CD
T-39

**e** Listen to five people talking about their experiences working in another culture. Take notes about the things that they found different or unusual in the business culture of the other country.

| home country / visiting | observations |
| --- | --- |
| China / USA: | |
| UK / Saudi Arabia: | |
| Japan / Brazil: | |
| USA / France: | |
| UAE / Australia: | |

**f** In pairs or small groups, discuss these questions.

1. Why do you think English has become the international language of business?
2. In which countries would someone from your country experience the most *culture shock?*
3. What aspects of your culture do foreigners often find it hard to get used to?
4. In which English-speaking country would you most like to study English. Why?

**g** As a way of improving your English, you have decided to subscribe to an Internet pen pal agency. The agency has provided you with the details of a person your age in the USA. In your notebook, write an informal letter including the following information.

- a brief introduction about yourself
- reason(s) why you want to improve your English
- a description of your current English classes
- brief explanation of the things that you find difficult in learning the language
- comments about how you try to overcome these difficulties

## Lesson 2

# Corporate culture

**a** In pairs or small groups, discuss the meaning of these expressions.

| management structure | organizational culture |
|---|---|

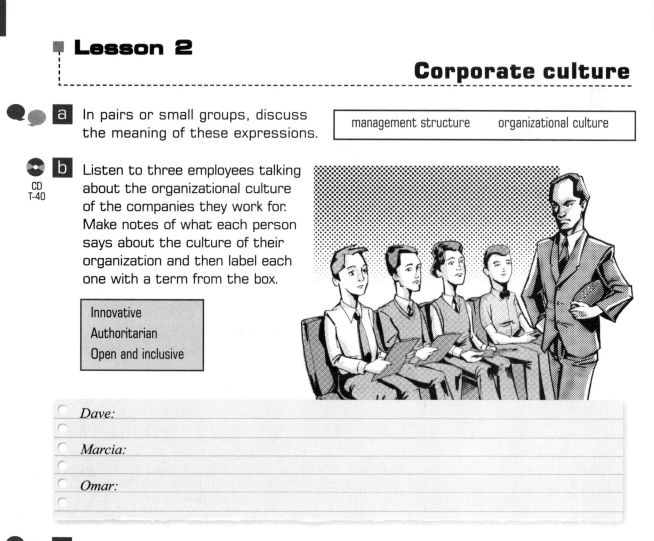

**b** Listen to three employees talking about the organizational culture of the companies they work for. Make notes of what each person says about the culture of their organization and then label each one with a term from the box.

CD
T-40

Innovative
Authoritarian
Open and inclusive

*Dave:*

*Marcia:*

*Omar:*

**c** Read about three different companies. Then, in pairs or small groups, discuss which types of organizational culture they exemplify.

**Winthrop Travel Agency** is a medium-sized business. Joel Grimes inherited the company from his father in 1994. He worked his way up and he understands all aspects of the travel industry. He likes to be totally involved and insists on interviewing all final interviewees for positions with the company. Recently, he seems to be having trouble keeping staff and there has been criticism of his management style. He is seen as being very controlling as he interferes in almost every aspect of the business.

**California Coolers** makes fruit drinks. Their directors encourage open and honest communication among the staff. Ideas are shared and everyone is encouraged to participate. The organization of office space reflects the company's philosophy. An open-plan system is used and everyone communicates freely because of the intermingling of staff from all departments. Employees are motivated because they feel appreciated and involved in what is happening in the company. To an outsider, this setup may appear to lack privacy and interfere with productivity, but it works very well.

**Worldwide Bank** is a large banking conglomerate that has a novel way of motivating its employees. Working with a well-known environmental group, they organize challenging projects for their employees. One project involved a trip to work with the crocodile population in the Okavanga Delta in Botswana. In this way, the bank tries to give employees a sense of how their lives and work relate to the environment. Upon returning, employees are encouraged to do something environmentally valuable in their own communities.

**d** Find words in the texts that mean the same as the following expressions.

1. to receive property, money, etc., from someone who has died (par. 1)  *inherit*

2. to order or demand firmly that something happen (par. 1)  _____

3. to take some action in a matter that does not concern you (par. 1)  _____

4. to give active approval and support for something (par. 2)  _____

5. to express, to make clear, to be a sign of (par. 2)  _____

6. a person not included in a certain group or organization (par. 2)  _____

7. new, clever, original (par. 3)  _____

8. difficult but in an interesting way (par. 3)  _____

**e** In pairs, discuss your reactions to what you read in the texts.

**f** Listen and write the letter of each sentence opening next to the correct ending.

CD
T-41

1. __*b*__     . . . and moving away from the command and control models of the past.

2. _____     . . . to collaborate and connect with other organizations.

3. _____     . . . in which different types of technology are employed together.

4. _____     . . . all staff can access corporate applications and information resources.

5. _____     . . . along with e-mails and other online transactions.

6. _____     . . . has evolved in some of the large corporations.

7. _____     . . . among many employees because of constant pressure and the change of pace.

**g** Role-play conversations in which a manager delegates the following tasks to an employee. Use the expressions in the box.

| | | |
|---|---|---|
| Could you arrange . . . | I would like you to . . . | Can you . . . |
| I need you to . . . | | Please call . . . |

A. The manager asks an employee to call the bank urgently to verify a bank statement as the one received does not match company accounts.

B. The manager asks an employee to check on the Internet for some information needed for a meeting the following day. This must be done immediately.

C. The manager asks an employee to contact all staff to inform them of a meeting next week. Specify that the manager must be informed if any staff cannot attend.

D. The manager asks an employee to research information on the best deals for website design. Detailed proposals from at least three designers are needed.

## Lesson 3

# Workplace changes

**a** Discuss these questions in pairs or small groups.

1. Do you prefer working with others or working alone?
2. What kinds of jobs can people do from home nowadays?
3. Do you know anyone who works from his/her home?
4. What are the pros and cons of working from home?

**b** Listen to three people discussing the advantages and disadvantages of working from home or in an office and take notes about their comments.

CD
T-42

| | *Working from home* | *Working in an office* |
|---|---|---|
| Marcus | | |
| Paula | | |
| Jake | | |

**c** Discuss these questions in pairs.

1. What you understand by the term *outsourcing?*
2. Do you know of any companies that outsource?
3. Why might a company decide to outsource some of its work?

**d** Read the article about outsourcing and underline five benefits that are mentioned.

In recent years, many companies have looked at ways of reducing the number of employees who carry out routine administrative tasks, and consequently they have outsourced such work to specialist companies that have more expertise and experience. Apart from administrative tasks, other work that is often outsourced is information technology support. Companies decide not to maintain IT departments of their own but, instead, they employ smaller, more specialized IT companies to provide the support they need, including, for example, e-mail management, backup, and storage. With outsourcing, the larger company not only cuts costs, but also gains the specialist knowledge of the smaller company. As a result, it keeps its systems up to date without spending time and money on staff training programs. In this way, outsourcing allows a company to focus on its core competencies—that is, to devote time and resources to what it does best.

However, outsourcing has its critics. Some point to a lack of loyalty to the larger company on the part of the service provider, while others have raised doubts about the quality of the service provided.

**e** Look at these connecting expressions from the text on the previous page. Label each one *contrast*, *cause and effect*, or *addition*.

1. apart from      *addition*
2. instead      _____
3. however      _____

4. as a result      _____
5. not only / but also      _____
6. consequently      _____

**f** Read the next part of the article and divide it into three paragraphs. Mark the place where you think the second and third paragraphs should begin.

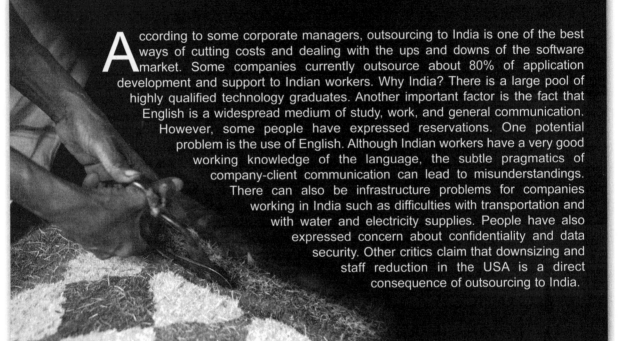

According to some corporate managers, outsourcing to India is one of the best ways of cutting costs and dealing with the ups and downs of the software market. Some companies currently outsource about 80% of application development and support to Indian workers. Why India? There is a large pool of highly qualified technology graduates. Another important factor is the fact that English is a widespread medium of study, work, and general communication. However, some people have expressed reservations. One potential problem is the use of English. Although Indian workers have a very good working knowledge of the language, the subtle pragmatics of company-client communication can lead to misunderstandings. There can also be infrastructure problems for companies working in India such as difficulties with transportation and with water and electricity supplies. People have also expressed concern about confidentiality and data security. Other critics claim that downsizing and staff reduction in the USA is a direct consequence of outsourcing to India.

**g** In your notebook, write notes in two columns summarizing the advantages and disadvantages of outsourcing to India.

**h** In pairs, role-play a conversation based on the following information.

**Student A**

You are a manager. Talk to your colleague, Student B, and try to convince him/her of the need to outsource human resources functions as a way of saving money.

**Student B**

You are a manager. Talk to your colleague, Student A, and try to persuade him/her not to outsource human resources functions because of your concerns about confidentiality and the quality of the service.

**i** Research information about other countries, for example, China, where outsourcing has become an important part of the economy. Prepare a written report to present to the rest of the class.

## Lesson 4
# The other side of modern business

**a** Look at the image and discuss the answers to these questions in pairs or small groups.

1. What do you know about this company?
2. What happened to it?
3. Do you know of any high-profile cases of corporate fraud in your country?
4. In your country, what government organization investigates cases of corporate fraud?

**b** Listen and complete the notes about Enron with the correct information.

CD
T-43

> **_Enron Corporation_**
> _energy company based in _____, Texas_
> _went bankrupt _____
> _before bankruptcy, employed around _____ people_
> _claimed revenues in 2000: _____ billion_
> _Fortune magazine -"America's Most Innovative Company" from _____ to 2001_
> _Fortune's "_____ Best Companies to Work for in America" _____
> _Enron bankruptcy biggest in U.S. history - _____ lost jobs_

**c** Read more information about the Enron Corporation and answer the questions.

Enron grew prosperous, so it claimed, through its pioneering marketing and promotion of power commodities and related derivatives in the form of tradable financial instruments. However, it was later discovered that Enron's reported financial situation was sustained mainly by institutionalized, systematic, and carefully planned accounting fraud. Investigations into Enron's irregular accounting practices revealed that many of its recorded assets and profits were illegally inflated or were completely nonexistent. Enron accountants carried out mysterious and improper financial transactions between the company and related "offshore" businesses. Enron had created these companies deliberately so that debts and losses from unprofitable entities were not included in the company's official financial statements. The Enron scandal was one of the biggest and most complex bankruptcy cases in U.S. history. It has since become an infamous symbol of willful corporate fraud and corruption.

1. What was the supposed source of Enron's enormous wealth?
2. What was the actual source of the company's wealth?
3. How did Enron cover up its debts and losses?

**d** Find words in the text that are the opposites of the following words.

1. legally    _____       4. existent    _____
2. profitable _____       5. proper      _____
3. regular    _____

**e** Complete the chart below with words that form their opposites with the given prefixes. Use the words in the box plus other words that you know.

| committal | rational | lawful | legible | discriminatory |
| possible | responsible | prudent | logical | truthful |

| il- | im- | ir- | non- | un- |
|---|---|---|---|---|
| *legible* | *possible* | | | |

**f** Read the text on the previous page again and find examples of the following verb structures. Write them below. Then, in pairs, analyze the use and function of each verb structure.

1. simple past            _____ *Investigations . . . revealed that . . .* _____
2. passive voice in the past   _____
3. past perfect           _____
4. present perfect        _____

**g** Complete the sentences with the correct form of the verb in parentheses.

1. Political events _____ (affect) the price of energy a lot since 2001.
2. After the Chernobyl disaster in 1985, the use of nuclear energy _____ (decline).
3. It was later discovered that the company _____ (inflated) its profits.
4. Do you think attitudes towards big business _____ (change) in recent years?

**h** In small groups, discuss the legal and moral responsibilities that you think corporations and governments have or should have toward consumers and the general public.

**i** Look for information about a recent high-profile case of corporate fraud and present your findings in an oral report to the rest of the class.

## Lesson 5
# Global concerns in the business world

**a** Look at the issues below and, from the perspective of an employee in a company, rate them in order of importance from 1 (most important) to 10 (least important).

health and safety ☐   energy problems ☐   pension plan ☐   training courses ☐   contract length ☐

pollution ☐   salary concerns ☐   outsourcing ☐   political events ☐   promotion prospects ☐

**b** Compare your ratings with those of a classmate.

**Example:**

I rate contract length as the most important issue. You put this as least important.

**c** Now get together in groups of four and report what you just discussed with your partner. Use the expressions in the boxes below to express opinions and to mark contrast.

**Example:**

In my opinion, political events are least important while salary concerns are the most important.

| expressing an opinion | expressing contrast |
| --- | --- |
| In my view/opinion, . . . | whereas |
| According to . . . | while |
| I believe that . . . | but |
| She is of the opinion that . . . | However, . . . |
| He thinks/argues/contends that . . . | On the other hand, . . . |

**d** Discuss these questions in pairs or small groups.

1. What experience have you had concerning the issues on this page?

2. How do you think employees can involve themselves in policy-making?

**e** Listen to a businessman and try to identify which industry he is describing.

CD
T-44

**f** Listen again and number the issues in the box in the order that they are mentioned.

CD
T-45

| | | | |
|---|---|---|---|
| fashion trends | ☐ | health and safety | ☐ |
| inflation | ☐ | labor costs | ☐ |
| marketing costs | ☐ | outsourcing | ☐ |
| people's tastes | ☐ | pollution control | ☐ |
| raw materials | ☐ | the competition | ☐ |

**g** In pairs or small groups, discuss the answers to these questions.

1. What is the price of oil at the moment?
2. Has the price gone up or come down in recent months?
3. What factors can cause the price of oil to increase or fall?

**h** Listen and make notes about changes in the price of oil over the last few years.

CD
T-46

**i** Use the data to draw a line graph in your notebook illustrating increases in the price of oil over time.

**j** Referring to the information in your graph, discuss with your classmates your predictions concerning the cost of oil over the next five years. Use the expressions in the box.

> The price of oil is going to continue rising . . .
>
> It is likely to go on increasing . . .
>
> It will probably decrease . . .
>
> It may/might continue to rise, but it depends on . . .

**k** Work in groups of four. First assign each member of your group one of the forms of energy from the box. Then research information and prepare an oral report about your chosen form of energy, outlining its advantages and disadvantages.

| | | | |
|---|---|---|---|
| hydrogen | solar | wind and wave | biomass |

**l** Share your information with the other members of your group. Be prepared to answer questions.

**m** As a group, decide on your preferred form of energy and summarize your reasons in a written report.

## Lesson 6

# Ethical trading

**a** Discuss these questions in pairs or small groups.

1. What is ethical trading?

2. Which companies have you heard of that could be called ethical companies?

3. n your country, how familiar are people generally with the concept of ethical trading?

**b** Read and complete each space in the article with the correct form of a word from the box.

| believe | capital | chemistry | ethics | grow | invest | profit | test |
|---------|---------|-----------|--------|------|--------|--------|------|

**What is ethical trading?** (1) _____*Ethical*_____ companies are usually set up by people with certain (2) _____ and principles. The aim is to be (3) _____ and to give people what they want, but without compromising these principles. These companies usually have strong beliefs regarding such issues as (4) _____, organic food, the environment, animal (5) _____, fair wages, and child labor.

**Why the sell-out now?** In the late 1990s, many investors, especially venture (6) _____, began shouting for a return on their (7) _____. For many of these ethical companies, going public was not a viable option. At the same time, the large multinationals saw the amazing (8) _____ and interest in organic and ethically traded goods. It was cheaper for them to buy an existing established ethical company than to set up their own.

THE BODY SHOP

**c** Listen to check your answers.

CD T-47

**d** Now listen and match each company with the multinational that acquired it.

CD T-48

| ethical company | | bought by |
|-----------------|---|-----------|
| 1. The Body Shop | ___*d*___ | a. Groupe Danon |
| 2. Tom's of Maine | _____ | b. Coca Cola |
| 3. Linda McCartney's Whole foods | _____ | c. Cadbury-Schw |
| 4. Ben & Jerry's Ice Cream | _____ | d. L'Oreal |
| 5. Green & Black's Chocolate | _____ | e. Colgate |
| 6. Odwalla Juice | _____ | f. Hain Celestial |
| 7. Stonyfield Farm Organic Yogurt | _____ | g. Unilever |

🗨🗨 **e** Study the bar chart and discuss the growth in fair trading from 1998 to 2005.

**f** Now read the article and answer the questions in your notebook.

The concept of ethical trading known as Fairtrade was established slowly from the late 1980s in order to give a decent deal to producers in the developing world of basic commodities such as coffee, sugar, and cocoa at a time when they were faced with a global crash in commodity prices. Organizations that are involved in Fairtrade guarantee that farmers are paid a minimum price that is enough to cover production costs of basic commodities whatever world prices may be at the time.

From a slow start, Fairtrade business has really taken off and product sales rose 40% in 2005 alone to a figure of $295 million. Though this is still only 0.1% of world trade, the trend is upward and this indicates that people are beginning to take social and environmental issues into consideration when buying products. Fairtrade labeled products are stocked not just in specialist stores but they also can be found in many large supermarkets. According to the

principles of Fairtrade, workers' rights and environmental protection must be taken into consideration. Other ethical issues to be resolved are the exploitation of migrant workers and cheap labor. However, fundamental to the trading is how goods are produced and how they are sold. It is hoped that through fair trading, the benefits of free trade are brought into the hands of the people who really need it most.

1. What sort of products are typically bought and sold under according to Fairtrade practices?

2. Where can Fairtrade labeled products be bought?

3. How much of all world commerce is Fairtrade commerce?

4. Apart from trading practices, what other concerns are covered by Fairtrade principles?

🗨🗨 **g** Look through the article and underline phrases that are in the passive voice. Then discuss in pairs why the passive voice is used in each instance.

**h** Read these comments made about ethical trading. Write each one in your notebook exactly as the person said it.

**Example:**

"Ethical trading has taken ten years to really get going."

Nancy Ryder, a researcher at Ethical Consumer magazine, said that ethical trading had taken ten years to really get going. She said that research showed that 50% of people recognized the Fairtrade mark and that it had huge potential for further growth. She also said that many people liked the idea and that now they could buy products at their local supermarket instead of going to a specialist whole-food supplier. She commented that retailers stocked Fairtrade products because they were flying off the shelves. She added that the big increase in demand for Fairtrade and organic Easter eggs this year showed how mainstream they were becoming.

# Team Project 5

## Task:
### Prepare a report about future business trends

You have been asked to prepare an article for a general interest magazine on the subject of future trends in corporate business.

With your team:

1. Choose two or three general fields to focus on, for example, manufacturing, transportation, retail, banking, technology, etc.

2. Visit large companies involved in your chosen areas of business and arrange to interview key personnel at these companies.

3. Try to obtain predictions, opinions, insights, etc., about the following topics:
   - global cultural issues
   - corporate culture
   - changes in the workplace
   - ethical issues

4. Present your findings to the rest of the class.

# Additional Resources

# Review 1

**A** Rewrite the conversation between the school counselor and Jake and Paula in more formal and polite language.

**Jake:** Hi, Mrs. Madison. How is your day going? Do you have a few minutes to talk?

(1) _____

**Mrs. Madison:** What's your problem? I'm rushing off to pick up my kid from his day care.

(2) _____

**Paula:** Well, we're having a bit of trouble. We don't know how to find some work for the summer. Do you have any ideas?

(3) _____

**Mrs. Madison:** This isn't the best time for me to talk about this topic. Have you had a look at the newspaper ads or talked to your family about available jobs?

(4) _____

**Jake:** We thought that since it's your job to give us advice and help, we would start with you. What do you think?

(5) _____

**Mrs. Madison:** You know you really should try to help yourself. Come and see me tomorrow at 10 a.m. and don't be late.

(6) _____

**Paula:** Fine. See you then. Bye.

(7) _____

**B** Match each of the phrasal verbs (with **fill**) to the appropriate meaning.

| Verb phrase | | Meaning |
|---|---|---|
| 1. fill in | _____ | a. give someone some information |
| 2. fill in for | _____ | b. fill a container to the top |
| 3. fill in on | _____ | c. put a missing word in a sentence |
| 4. fill out | _____ | d. substitute for someone at work |
| 5. fill up | _____ | e. complete a form |

**C** Write questions for the following answers.

1. _____

Yes, I can swim but not very well.

2. _____

No, John doesn't have to attend the meeting this evening.

3. _____

Yes, Magda will probably drop by on her way home from work.

4. _____

Yes, she used to visit regularly last year.

5. _____

If she studies, she will definitely do well in the exam.

# Review 2

**A** Match the contrasting parts of each sentence. Then write the complete sentences using one of the linking words from the box.

| but | though | on the other hand | while | whereas |
|-----|--------|-------------------|-------|---------|

1. Many Internet companies were set up      _____
2. People let shops know when they are unhappy with a product      _____
3. A letter or phone call gives limited information about a candidate      _____
4. Both products were launched at the same time      _____
5. Work in the future will be quite different from what it is at the present      _____
6. We cannot normally choose when to receive a phone call      _____

a. they rarely return to say they are happy with a product.

b. an interview allows the employer to meet the interviewee face to face.

c. it is unlikely that it will be any less stressful than it is at the moment.

d. we can usually choose when to read an e-mail.

e. not all of them were successful.

f. the performance of both has been quite different.

1. _____
2. _____
3. _____
4. _____
5. _____
6. _____

**B** Complete the sentences with the correct form of the verbs below.

| pick up on | build on | tune into | turn out |
|------------|----------|-----------|----------|

1. The event _____ to be a great success.
2. Online communication with customers _____ the problems they were experiencing.
3. The new employee _____ what the department expected of him.
4. The company needs to _____ previous marketing strategies.

**C** Complete the conditional sentences with the correct form of the verb in parentheses.

1. If you _____ (want) to succeed in your career, you must work hard.
2. If a businessman _____ (set up) a new business, he has to give it a catchy name.
3. If world trade and globalization _____ (generate) confidence, they observe responsible business practices.
4. If the student _____ (use) his credit card carefully, he doesn't run up a lot of debt.
5. If the marketing department _____ (be) successful, it understands the target market.

# Review 3

**A** Complete the conversation with the correct passive form of the verb in parentheses.

Secretary: Do you think we can market the product on time for the holiday?
Manager: Yes, it (1) _____ (can / market) on time if we all work together.
Secretary: Will we prepare an advertising campaign?
Manager: Yes, an ad campaign (2) _____ (design) next week.
Secretary: Who invented the product?
Manager: It (3) _____ (invent) by a designer from an associate company.
Secretary: Who conducted the market survey?
Manager: The research (4) _____ (carry out) by the company's marketing team.

**B** Write a persuasive statement for each situation using the modals *must, ought to,* or *should.*

1. Persuade your friend to go to the cinema with you tonight.

   _____

2. Convince the manager that it is better to postpone the marketing meeting.

   _____

3. Persuade a colleague to work overtime to finish an important project.

   _____

4. Try to persuade a customer to buy a product that your company is selling.

   _____

5. Convince a colleague to help you fix your computer.

   _____

**C** Complete the sentences with the *present perfect, present simple,* or *past simple* tense form of the verb in parentheses.

1. Although, the company _____ (exceed) sales expectations last year they _____ (not reach) their quote so far this year.
2. Pedro _____ (work) in Intel. He _____ (work) since 1998.
3. The manager _____ (just arrive) and he _____ (want) to speak to all the staff. It _____ (sound) urgent.
4. John _____ (go) to the office early this morning. Ten hours later he _____ (be) still there. He _____ (not have) lunch and he _____ (not yet eat) dinner.

**D** Complete the following sentences with forms of comparison.

1. Bill Gates is _____ successful _____ Larry Klein.
2. Clubs are _____ popular _____ movie theaters.
3. African crafts are not _____ well-known _____ Latin American crafts.
4. The secretary works _____ hard _____ as her supervisors.
5. The office computer is _____ powerful _____ your laptop.

# Review 4

**A**   Write the necessary question for each one of the situations below.

1. You've forgotten when the meeting begins. Ask a colleague.

   _____

2. The staff party is on Friday. Ask a friend how much it costs to go.

   _____

3. You have just joined a new company. Ask another employee how many people work in the marketing department.

   _____

4. The manager has just called a meeting. Ask a colleague why you have to go.

   _____

5. The supervisor wants one of the reports on the shelf. Ask her which report she needs.

   _____

**B**   Write sentences that reflect your thoughts about your expenditures for a trip you would like to take.

1. I need to figure out _____
2. I should plan _____
3. I'll probably need _____
4. I'll have to stay _____
5. I may need to borrow _____
6. I'll definitely have to cut down on _____

**C**   Use the words and phrases in the box to complete the sentences.

| bear in mind | placement | trustworthy | maximize your profits | do your homework |
|---|---|---|---|---|

1. When deciding on a purchase of goods, you need to _____ the cost.
2. The new IT company seems _____.
3. I think this investment will _____.
4. You really need to _____ before making an important decision.
5. The broker assured me that the _____ of the order went through.

# Review 5

**A** Complete the exchanges by writing the correct form of the verbs in parentheses.

1. **A:** _____ (you / meet) your friend at the conference last week?
   **B:** No, she _____ (leave) by the time I _____ (arrive).
2. **A:** The manager _____ (look) for you a few minutes ago.
   **B:** Thanks. I _____ (just talk) with him. He _____ (want) me to meet an important client this afternoon.
3. **A:** More and more companies _____ (go) virtual these days. People are in different locations and _____ (use) electronic communication tools to collaborate.
   **B:** I hear it saves a lot of time because virtual teams _____ (not engage) in causal conversation and _____ (not waste) time.
4. **A:** The stock market _____ (close) at an unexpected high at 6 p.m. today.
   **B:** I heard that the continuous higher than expected sales at Café Now _____ (help) the dramatic rise.

**B** Complete the sentences with the correct phrasal verb from the box.

| tune in |
| catch on |
| get in on |
| turn out |
| work out |
| get on |

1. The new computer technician didn't _____ to the procedures immediately.
2. The administrator _____ very well with his staff.
3. The designers have to _____ continuously to the new trends.
4. The sales department _____ new strategies for distribution.
5. The design of the bottle _____ to be quite original.
6. The marketing department _____ the competition's marketing strategies.

**C** Report the following statements. They were all spoken in the past. Use the verbs in parentheses.

1. Secretary to manager: Don't forget to sign the report. (remind)
   _The secretary reminded the manager to sign the report._
2. Jackie: I'm sorry I missed the meeting yesterday. (apologize)
   _____
3. Supervisor: Did someone phone while I was out? (ask)
   _____
4. Simon: Why don't we go out for lunch today? (suggest)
   _____
5. Manager: Have the report ready by three o' clock. (order)
   _____
6. Janet: Can I leave early this afternoon? (ask permission)
   _____

# Making suggestions

| Suggestion | Example |
|---|---|
| Negative *wh-* questions | **Why don't** we go to the movies? |
| We could | **We could** go out to eat tonight. |
| I suggest | **I suggest** we buy John a birthday present. |
| Let's | **Let's** talk to the boss about a new computer. |
| I think | **I think** it's time we took a break. We've been at this for two hours. |
| We should think about/consider | **We should think about** finishing the project today. **We should consider** finishing the project today. |
| Maybe we should | **Maybe we should** have a meeting about . . . |

 **Note:** There are many ways to make suggestions in English. Notice the grammatical form that is appropriate with each phrase.

## PRACTICE

Make suggestions for the situations below. Use the word or phrase in parentheses.

1. Invite employees from the Finance Department to the meeting (Why don't)

   _____

2. Rent the conference room in hotel for gathering. (could)

   _____

3. Interview only five applicants for position of secretary. (suggest)

   _____

4. Start the interviews at 9 a.m. (consider/think about)

   _____

5. Time off to prepare for conference. (Let's)

   _____

6. Have a lunch meeting. (think about)

   _____

7. Get an additional secretary. (consider/think)

   _____

8. Have a quick meeting to discuss procedures. (Maybe)

   _____

## ABOUT YOU

Write three suggestions that you would make to your supervisor at work or at school.

1. _____

2. _____

3. _____

## Giving advice

### Examples

**I think you should** consider taking a course in Human Resources Management.

**It's a good idea to** plan ahead and consider your options.

**I would advise you to** find out as much as you can about each department.

**My advice to you is to** do plenty of research on the company before going for an interview.

**If I were you**, I would call the office and ask about the job.

**Whatever you do don't** tell them you may resign if you find a better job.

**It is advisable to** prepare yourself for an interview.

**Note:** There are a number of ways to give a person advice. Look at the above and note the sentence structure in each example.

### PRACTICE

Use expressions from the examples above to give advice to a person in the following situations.

1. Advise a friend not to work too hard.

   _____

2. Give a friend advice on how to prepare for an interview.

   _____

3. Advise a friend about applying for a job.

   _____

4. Give a friend advice on the best way to prepare for a university examination.

   _____

5. Give a friend advice on how to learn to use a design program on the computer.

   _____

### ABOUT YOU

Write four situations related to persons in your work or family environment that require advice. Then write sentences about what you would say to them.

_____  _____  _____  _____

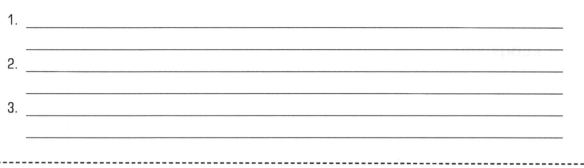

1. _____

   _____

2. _____

   _____

3. _____

   _____

# Phrasal verbs

| Suggestion | Explanation |
|---|---|
| The secretary <u>took down</u> the information.<br>The company had to <u>cut back</u> on spending. | Verb + preposition/adverb |
| The manager <u>called</u> him <u>in</u> to <u>sort</u> the financial difficulties <u>out</u>. | Sometimes the parts of the phrasal verb can be separated by a noun or pronoun. |
| I couldn't <u>keep up with</u> the new information. | Three-word phrasal verbs cannot be separated by a noun or pronoun. |

 **Note:** Phrasal verbs consist of a two- to three-word phrase rather than a single word. The group of words creates a new meaning.

## PRACTICE

Check ✓ the sentences where the word order is correct.

_____ The HR department looked the new employees after.

_____ The secretary called up security to investigate the noises.

_____ The management came up some difficulties against in their attempts to take over the company.

_____ The messenger handed the packages over to the receptionist.

_____ It didn't take long to clear the mess up.

_____ The sudden drop in share prices has given rise speculation to among the shareholders.

# Collocations

A collocation refers to a group of words that are often found together. Combine words/phrases from Box A with words/phrases from Box B to form natural collocations.

| A | balance   business   launch   stiff   achieve   annual   customer   booming<br>keep   give   successful   make   fulfilling   submit   apply for |
|---|---|
| B | a new product   a partnership      a career in business   a job   copies<br>a record   a presentation   turnover   service   instructions   decisions<br>business   (the) budget   competition   goals |

1. _____    5. _____    9. _____

2. _____    6. _____    10. _____

3. _____    7. _____    11. _____

4. _____    8. _____    12. _____

## ABOUT YOU

Write three sentences that are true for you using some of the collocations you made.

1. _____

2. _____

3. _____

## Expressing obligation

| Example | Explanation |
|---|---|
| I **have to** work late tonight to finish the report. | Use *have to* to show obligation. |
| Jim **must** buy a new laptop with more memory. | Use *must* to indicate that something is necessary. |
| You **should** take a course in Web Design.<br>You **ought to** take a course—you will enjoy it. | Use *should/ought to* to describe what the best or right thing to do is—closer to advice. |
| We **need to** look more carefully at their performance record. | Use *need to* to show that something is essential or extremely important |

**Note:** There are a number of ways to express obligation. Look at the above and note the sentence structure in each example.

### PRACTICE
Use an expression of obligation to complete the following statements.

1. You / wear protective clothing / when you go into the electrical room.

   _____

2. You / supply referees who know your work performance / when you submit your CV.

   _____

3. I / take some courses from time to time / stay up-to-date with the latest knowledge.

   _____

4. I / buy the *Financial Times* because it has information on the shares.

   _____

5. She is sitting there doing nothing. She / be working.

   _____

### ABOUT YOU
Write five sentences that express obligations related to work, school or family/social/ financial responsibilities that are true for you.

1. _____
2. _____
3. _____
4. _____
5. _____

# Real conditionals in the future

## Condition

| Condition<br>*If* + subject + present tense verb | Result<br>subject + *will* + verb |
| --- | --- |
| If we invest the money in real estate,<br>If the company offers me a job, | we will make a good profit.<br>I will accept it. |

## *Yes/no* questions

| *If* + subject + present tense verb | *will* + subject + verb ? |
| --- | --- |
| If we invest the money in real estate,<br>If the company offers you a job, | will we make a good profit?<br>will you accept it? |

## *Wh-* questions

| *If* + subject + present tense verb | *wh-* word + *will* + subject + verb ? |
| --- | --- |
| If we reduce monthly expenses,<br>If the company lays off workers, | how much will we save?<br>what will they do? |

- Real conditionals describe future situations that are real or possible under certain circumstances. The *if* clause describes a condition, while the main clause describes a certain or probable result.
- The *if* clause can come first or second in the sentence.
    - I'll talk to the IT team *if* I have time this week.
    - *If* I have time this week, I'll talk to the design team.
- When the *if* clause comes first in a sentence, it is followed by a comma.

## PRACTICE
Complete the sentences with the correct form of the verb.

1. If companies _____ (think) carefully about their advertising, their share of the market _____ (will increase) considerably.

2. If marketing employees _____ (design) a successful ad campaign, _____ they _____ (succeed) in selling their products?

3. If a businessman _____ (use) his own name as a brand, it _____ (indicate) a desire to personalize his product.

4. If the store _____ (locate) the goods in a prominent position, what _____ (happen)?

5. If the company _____ (start) a small and concentrated publicity campaign, it _____ (be) more successful.

## ▪ Word forms

Some expressions used to describe trends can occur as nouns and adjectives or verbs and adverbs. Look at the sentences below and note the changes in parts of speech.

### PRACTICE

Complete the columns with words or phrases to make a logical sentence. Then use different sentences to describe the events in the graph below.

|  | Adjective | Noun |  |
|---|---|---|---|
| There was a | slight<br>gradual<br>sudden<br>steady<br>sharp<br>dramatic | decline<br>fall<br>drop<br>dip<br>increase<br>rise | in sales.<br>in profits.<br>(1) _____<br>(2) _____<br>(3) _____ |

|  | Verb | Adverb |
|---|---|---|
| Profits<br>(4) _____<br>(5) _____<br>(6) _____ | declined<br>fell<br>dropped<br>dipped<br>increased<br>rose | sharply.<br>steadily.<br>slightly.<br>gradually.<br>dramatically.<br>suddenly.<br>unexpectedly. |

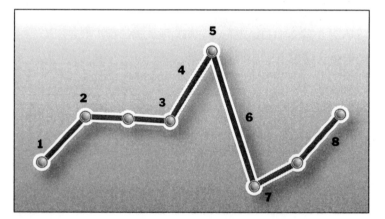

1. _____
2. _____
3. _____
4. _____
5. _____
6. _____
7. _____
8. _____

# Passive voice

| Passive voice | Form |
|---|---|
| Affirmative statement | Subject + *be* + past participle + complement<br>A product is marketed for the target population. |
| Negative statement | Subject + *be* + *not* + past participle + complement<br>The product is not delivered immediately. |
| *Yes/no* question | *Be* + subject + past participle + complement<br>Is the market identified during the first phase? |
| *Wh-* questions | *Wh-* word + *be* + subject + past participle + complement<br>When is the product taken off the market? |

- The passive voice is used to give more emphasis to an action rather than to the person or thing that performs the action. We use the passive voice when the subject is less important, or when it is implicitly understood or is not known.
- Passive sentences usually sound more formal than active ones.
- The passive voice is commonly used in news reports, official documents, descriptions of processes, etc.
- The agent (doer of the action) may or may not be included in a passive voice sentence. If it is, it is introduced with *by*.

## PRACTICE 1
Rewrite the sentences using the passive voice.

1. The committee selects the most competent candidate.
   _____

2. The planned merger prolongs the life of the company.
   _____

3. We will market the new product as soon as we have a firm plan.
   _____

4. The company bought the building in 1985 and expanded it to its present size.
   _____

5. The director hired Jonas as a troubleshooter for the computer department.
   _____

## PRACTICE 2
Complete the sentences with the active or passive verb as needed.

1. Organic retail outlets _____ (pay) farmers a fair wage for their products.
2. The idea of ethical trading _____ (establish) to make sure producers get a decent return on their products.
3. The difficulties between the employees _____ (resolve) at a meeting.

# Expressing possibility

### Examples

Many small companies **are likely to** go out of business if energy costs continue to rise.
People **generally** like to think about a purchase before buying.
Credit cards **can be** a problem if you are an impulse shopper.
It **may be** difficult to balance the budget in times of rising prices.
Young people **are likely to** be attracted to a job that pays well and has promotion prospects.

## PRACTICE

Use expressions from the examples above to write sentences that describe possibility in the following situations.

1. The kind of person who makes a good manager or supervisor.

2. How rising travel prices might affect people's ability to take a holiday.

3. How increasing global warming concerns could affect business.

4. How a new company selling the same product as yours might affect your business.

5. How falling share prices might affect people's confidence in the stock market.


# Making polite requests

### Examples

**Can** you let me know when Jack arrives?
**Could** you give me a call when the report is ready?
**Would you mind** letting me know when Sonya telephones?

## PRACTICE

Make polite requests for the situations below.

1. You want an employee to tell you when the report is ready.

2. You want a copy of the latest catalog.

3. You want the stapler.

4. You want the music turned down.

5. You want the staff to be available for the meeting at 5 p.m.

## Simple vs. continuous tenses

| Example | Explanation | Superlative |
|---|---|---|
| The earth **revolves** around the sun. | Use the simple present to talk about regular or habitual activities and scientific truths. | the fastest |
| | | the nicest |
| Fabian **drives** to work every day. | | the biggest |
| | | the noisiest |
| Fabian **is attending** a workshop. | Use the present continuous to talk about an action in progress at the time of speaking. | the most modern |
| | | the best |
| | | the worst |
| | | the farthest |

### PRACTICE
Complete the sentences with the correct form of the verb in parentheses.

1. I'm afraid you can't see the manager right now. He _____ (meet) with Joe Clarke.
2. Successful investors generally _____ (invest) money in a variety of options.
3. Xavier _____ (own) the largest accountancy firm in the country and _____ (plan) to expand overseas.
4. Interests rates _____ (rise) and homeowners are concerned about their repayments.
5. We _____ (pay) the price now for not moving quickly on the deal.

## Simple past vs. past continuous tense

| Example | Explanation |
|---|---|
| **He** negotiated a loan with the bank to purchase the property. | Use the simple past to talk about actions that happened in the past and are completed. |
| He **was negotiating** a loan with the bank when the manager changed his mind. | Use the past continuous to talk about an action in progress at a stated time in the past. It generally occurs with the past simple to show that one action was in progress when another happened. |

### PRACTICE
Complete the sentences with the correct form of the verb in parentheses.

1. Anthony _____ (work) with MTP at first but _____ (set up) his own company in 1989.
2. James _____ (set up) a joint venture with another construction company but _____ (change) his mind because of differences of opinion.
3. Michael Birch, founder of Bebo website, _____ (not make) any money in London so he _____ (move) to California in 2002 and has become a very successful entrepreneur.
4. The young programmer _____ (lack) the money but not the initiative to do well

# Comparative and superlative forms of adjectives

| Type of adjectives | Simple form | Comparative | |
|---|---|---|---|
| one syllable | fast | faster | |
| one syllable ending in -e | nice | nicer | |
| ending in consonant + vowel + consonant | big | bigger | |
| ending in -y | noisy | noisier | |
| two or more syllables | modern | more modern | |
| irregular | good<br>bad<br>far | better<br>worse<br>farther | |

- Use the comparative form to compare two objects or persons.
- If the second **object** or **person** is mentioned in the comparison, use *than* before it.
- Use the superlative form to compare a group of objects or persons.
- Use *the* before superlative adjectives.

## PRACTICE 1
Write the comparative and superlative form of each adjective.

1. elegant _____
2. hard _____
3. intelligent _____
4. lazy _____
5. small _____

6. difficult _____
7. useful _____
8. good _____
9. practical _____
10. inexpensive _____

## PRACTICE 2
Use the cues to write sentences making comparisons.

1. Working in marketing / interesting working in finance

_____

2. Communicating through Internet / efficient / writing a letter

_____

3. Old office / small and cramped / new office

_____

4. Investing in stocks and shares / risky / government bonds

_____

5. Laptops / expensive / personal computers

_____

# Present perfect vs. simple past

| Present perfect | |
|---|---|
| Affirmative statement | The manager has talked to the employees about the issue many times. <br> subject + *has/have* + past participle |
| Negative statement | He has not worked in a foreign country before. <br> subject + *has/have* + *not* + past participle |
| *Yes/no* questions | Have you taken any finance courses? <br> *has/have* + subject + past participle |
| *Wh-* questions | How long has the project been a success? <br> *Wh-* word + *has/have* + subject + past participle |

Use the present perfect tense:
- to show that something happened at an unspecified time in the past.
- to show that something happened several times in the past.
- to show that something started at a specific time in the past and continues now.

## PRACTICE 1

Complete the conversation with the present perfect form of each verb in parentheses.

**Mr. Scott:**      ___*Have you finished*___ (finish) all the reports?

**Mrs. Baldwin:** No, I (1) _____ (finish / not) them yet.

**Mr. Scott:** You don't have to go to the bank. I (2) _____ (already get) some foreign money.

**Mrs. Baldwin:** Great! (3) _____ you _____ (pick up) the plane tickets?

**Mr. Scott:** No, and I (4) _____ (not / download) the presentation for the meeting yet.

**Mrs. Baldwin:** Don't forget to pack your laptop as well!

## PRACTICE 2

Complete each the sentence with the correct form of the verb in the present perfect or simple past.

1. The online chat rooms _____ (generate) a huge amount of money up to the present.

2. Birch _____ (remortgage) his house last year  to cover the initial costs of setting up his business.

3. The website _____ (grow) exponentially since it was first set up.

4. Some people argue that shopping malls _____ (destroy) the individual character of towns and shopping areas.

# Defining relative clauses

| Main clause | Adjective clause |
|---|---|
| Some work is done by private companies | **that** employ advertising experts. |
| This is the professor | **whose** students won the Innovation Award. |
| This is the place | **where** decisions about funding are taken. |
| This is the kind of employee | **who** is an independent decision maker. |
| A position with a strong personal development aspect is | **what** I am looking for. |

- A defining relative clause identifies a person or a thing.
- *Who, that, what, where,* and *whose* are relative pronouns.
- The relative pronoun *that* is often used instead of *who* or *which*.
- The relative pronoun *where* is used to refer to places.
- The possessive pronoun *whose* is usually used to refer to people. It is always followed by a noun.

## PRACTICE

Combine the two sentences using a relative pronoun.

1. Frank plans to invest more in marketing his products. His designs have been very popular.

   _____

2. The report was very well received. The report was prepared by the sales staff.

   _____

3. Michael lost money initially. He now runs a very successful website.

   _____

4. Shares have increased in value over the last ten months. The shares were bought in 2000.

   _____

5. The department has no more resources for the project. That is the difficult thing.

   _____

6. The new IT program is very complex. We have to follow the new IT program.

   _____

# Vocabulary for Business

| | | Unit | Meaning | Example |
|---|---|---|---|---|
| **absenteeism** | *n* | 1 | the fact or habit of frequently being away from work or school usually without a good reason | There has been a high rate of absenteeism over the last couple of months.<br><br>*absenteeism due to*<br>*absenteeism and tardiness* |
| **acquisition** | *n* | 5 | the act of getting or being given something | The acquisition of the property made it easier to establish the factory.<br><br>*acquisition of assets*<br>*acquisition of stock* |
| **adjustment** | *n* | 5 | an alteration or correction of something | Some adjustments had to be made in the system of payments after revision of the tax laws.<br><br>*structural adjustment*<br>*debt adjustment* |
| **after-sales** | *adj.* | 2 | taking place after a sale | The after-sales service of that company is not very good so I won't buy from them.<br><br>*after-sales follow-up* |
| **appraisal** | *n* | 1 | a careful judgment of how the employee is doing and how she/he can improve | The supervisor made a balanced appraisal of the new employee after a couple of months.<br><br>*performance appraisal*<br>*doing an appraisal* |
| **apprenticeship** | *n* | 1 | a period of time spent with a person who has a particular skill in order to learn the skill | He served a five-year apprenticeship before setting up his own business.<br><br>*to serve an apprenticeship*<br>*to do an apprenticeship* |
| **backlog** | *n* | 2 | a large amount of something or a large number of things that have accumulated and that must be dealt with | There is a huge backlog of mail that needs to be answered.<br><br>*backlog of*<br>*large backlog* |
| **balance** | *n* | 4 | the amount of money that remains after some of it has been spent | After he had paid all his bills he checked the balance in his account.<br><br>*account balance*<br>*bank balance* |
| **barrage** | *n* | 5 | a great number of questions, complaints, etc. | He faced a huge barrage of complaints after the poor decisions he made.<br><br>*barrage of questions*<br>*barrage of complaints* |
| **bidder** | *n* | 2 | a person who offers to pay a particular amount of money for an item | There was great interest in the property, and it was eventually sold to the highest bidder. |
| **brief** | *v* | 3 | to give someone information that they need or instructions before they do or deal with something | The marketing manager held a meeting to brief the employees about the new marketing plan. |
| **bulk** | *n* | 2 | a large quantity of something packaged to save money on individual items | The receptionist buys stationery in bulk as it saves time and money for her.<br><br>*bulk-buying*<br>*buy in bulk* |
| **bureaucratic** | *adj* | 5 | relating to rules and procedures that can cause long delays | There are so many bureaucratic procedures to follow that I feel the work will never be completed.<br><br>*bureaucratic system*<br>*bureaucratic complications* |

| | | Unit | Meaning | Example |
|---|---|---|---|---|
| **capacity** | *n* | 3 | the level of production in a factory or industry and the quantity of things that are produced | The company needs to raise its productivity and expand capacity if it wants to be successful. |
| **cash flow** | *n* | 4 | the movement of money in and out of a company | The company is having cash flow problems as more money is going out than is coming in.<br><br>*cash flow problems*<br>*projected cash flow* |
| **casualty** | *n* | 5 | a person or thing that has suffered badly as a result of a particular event or situation | Honesty was the first casualty in the negotiations between the two companies. |
| **ceiling** | *n* | 2 | an official upper limit on process and wages decided by the government or an organization | The banks are calling for a ceiling on mortgage rate increases.<br><br>*ceiling on wages*<br>*ceiling on interest rates* |
| **collaborate** | *v* | 5 | to work together to produce a piece of work or product | Jake and Kris collaborated on the design of the new merchandise.<br><br>*collaborate with*<br>*collaborate on* |
| **collapse** | *v* | 5 | to fail completely | Talks between the two groups collapsed after a few days because they could not find any common ground.<br><br>*the talks collapsed*<br>*the negotiations collapsed* |
| **collateral** | *n* | 4 | money or property that is used as a guarantee that someone will repay a loan | The young graduates wanted to set up their own business but they had nothing to offer as collateral.<br><br>*to put up collateral*<br>*to offer as collateral* |
| **commercial** | *adj* | 1 | involving or relating to commerce or business | He hopes to get a position with a commercial organization when he completes his training.<br><br>*commercial success/failure*<br>*commercial traveler/vehicle* |
| **commission** | *n* | 2 | a sum of money paid to a salesman for every sale that he/she makes | Salespeople generally get a sales commission on top of their basic salary.<br><br>*sales commission*<br>*paid by commission* |
| **concessions** | *n* | 2 | special rights or privileges that are given to someone | The oil company was granted concessions to explore for and develop the oil fields. |
| **conglomerate** | *n* | 5 | a large business firm consisting of several different companies that have joined together | A conglomerate is difficult to work in because it is so big and impersonal.<br><br>*media conglomerates*<br>*steel conglomerates* |
| **credentials** | *n* | 1 | a person's previous achievements, training and general background that indicate that the person is qualified to do something | His credentials indicated that he was the most suitable person for the job so we hired him.<br><br>*establish his credentials*<br>*show his credentials* |
| **cut-throat** | *adj* | 3 | behavior in which people want the same thing and do not care if they harm each other in getting it | The friends found it was a cut-throat business with a lot of interests involved and they couldn't succeed.<br><br>*cut-throat competition*<br>*cut-throat business* |

| | | Unit | Meaning | Example |
|---|---|---|---|---|
| **database** | *n* | 2 | a collection of data stored in a computer that enables people to get information very quickly | Data specialists refine lists of names and addresses in the database to improve market targeting.<br><br>*set up a database*<br>*search the database* |
| **deadline** | *n* | 2 | time or date before which a particular job or task must be finished | Mike felt stressed as he tried to finish the report for the Wednesday deadline.<br><br>*set deadlines*<br>*meet a deadline* |
| **defect** | *n* | 2 | a fault, flaw, or imperfection in a person or thing | Some of the devices were perfect but some had some small defects.<br><br>*slight defect*<br>*product defect* |
| **deteriorate** | *v* | 4 | to become worse in condition or quality | The economic state of the company continued to deteriorate in spite of efforts to improve things.<br><br>*deteriorating situation* |
| **disclosure** | *n* | 4 | the act of letting people know information that was originally secret | The disclosure of the disastrous financial condition of the company worried several staff members. |
| **dismissal** | *n* | 1 | the act of telling an employee that he/she is no longer needed to do the job that he/she has been doing | His dismissal came as a complete shock and he demanded to see the manager to discuss it.<br><br>*unfair dismissal* |
| **diversify** | *v* | 4 | to increase the variety of something that is made | The manufacturers realized that the only way to survive was to diversify their products. |
| **driven** | *adj* | 1 | motivated and persistent enough to try new things and to do them well | She is so energetic and driven in her work that she makes the rest of us look very lazy. |
| **empirical** | *adj* | 3 | relying on practical experience rather than theories | The theories need to be tested empirically before any decisions are made.<br><br>*empirical study*<br>*empirical research* |
| **endorse** | *v* | 3 | to give support or approval to someone | Management staff will be asked to endorse the new plans for expansion<br><br>*endorse the plans*<br>*endorse the product* |
| **enhance** | *v* | 2 | to improve the value, quality, or attractiveness of something | John's performance at the conference enhanced his reputation.<br><br>*enhance ability*<br>*enhance reputation* |
| **entity** | *n* | 5 | a complete, separate thing that is not divided or part of anything else | The company branched out on its own and became a separate entity.<br><br>*separate entity*<br>*an entity in its own right* |
| **escalating** | *adj* | 5 | becoming greater in size, seriousness, or intensity | There is a danger of escalating disagreement and then it will be extremely difficult to find a solution.<br><br>*escalating prices*<br>*escalating tensions* |

| | | Unit | Meaning | Example |
|---|---|---|---|---|
| **expenditure** | *n* | 4 | the amount of money that is spent on a particular thing or a particular situation | The marketing department has had to cut down their expenditure on the ad campaign.<br>*to cut down expenditure*<br>*minimum expenditure*<br>*cash expenditures* |
| **expertise** | *n* | 5 | a special skill or knowledge that is acquired by training, study or practice | His professional expertise has made a huge difference to the company. |
| **external** | *adj* | 4 | coming from the outside | External auditors were invited in to audit the accounts. |
| **facilitate** | *v* | 5 | to make it easier for an action or process to happen | The conference was rearranged to facilitate the arrival of delegates from overseas.<br>*facilitate planning*<br>*facilitate a meeting* |
| **fake** | *adj* | 3 | not genuine, made to trick people into thinking that something is genuine | This bag looks like the genuine item but there are some signs that indicate that it is a fake.<br>*fake goods*<br>*fake products* |
| **feedback** | *n* | 1 | comments and information about something that someone has made to tell whether it was liked or not | The more feedback the marketing department gets on the new product the better.<br>*positive feedback*<br>*negative feedback* |
| **fiscal** | *adj* | 4 | describing government or public money | Fiscal policies seriously affected the finances of the company.<br>*fiscal policies*<br>*fiscal year* |
| **fixed** | *adj* | 4 | remaining generally the same such as the cost of rent and utilities | The fixed costs are easy to keep track of; the fluctuating costs are more problematic.<br>*fixed costs*<br>*fixed expenditure* |
| **flagship** | *n* | 3 | the most important asset that a company has | The company has made changes to its new flagship product in order to satisfy the regulators. |
| **fluctuate** | *v* | 4 | to change the rate, speed, or cost of something quickly and irregularly | Prices fluctuated over a three-year period before finally stabilizing at $20 a share.<br>*supply and demand fluctuated* |
| **forecast** | *n* | 4 | a prediction or statement of what is expected to happen in the future | The profit forecasts for the coming year look very good.<br>*sales/trends/ developments forecast* |
| **freeze** | *n* | 1 | a halt in increases for a fixed period of time | The company was in financial difficulties and the employees agreed on a wage freeze for 24 months.<br>*price freeze*<br>*pay freeze* |
| **generate** | *v* | 4 | to cause a product or financial gain to be produced over a period of time | Increased investment in the company generated increased revenues over the year.<br>*generate income* |
| **impending** | *adj* | 5 | happening or appearing soon | The staff was aware of the impending danger to their company but were helpless to do anything about it.<br>*impending takeover*<br>*impending talks* |
| **implication** | *n* | 5 | something that is suggested or implied by a particular event, situation, or statement | The economic downturn had serious implications for the future of the country.<br>*negative implications*<br>*positive implications* |

| | | Unit | Meaning | Example |
|---|---|---|---|---|
| **impulsive** | *adj* | 2 | doing things suddenly without thinking about them carefully first | John's behavior can be quite impulsive so he was not given a lot of responsibility. *impulsive behavior* *impulsive personality* |
| **incentive** | *n* | 2 | something that encourages you to do something | There are few incentives to investing more money in the business as there is little chance of a good return on the money. *incentive to do something* *performance incentive* |
| **integrate** | *v* | 5 | to bring someone into the dominant group | It is important that new employees should be integrated into the existing group so their contribution will be positive. |
| **intermediary** | *n* | 4 | a person who tries to create agreement or pass information between two groups by talking to both | He acted as intermediary between the divided workers in the labor dispute. |
| **internal** | *adj* | 4 | happening inside a particular place | Internal disagreements were disrupting the smooth operation of the office. *internal disputes* *internal agreements* |
| **introvert** | *n* | 1 | someone who spends more time thinking of him/herself than about the world; someone who often finds it difficult to talk to other people | It may be difficult for a person who is considered an introvert to make a success of a job in sales. |
| **launch** | *v* | 3 | to make a new product available to the public | The new product was launched a couple of weeks ago and is already selling well. *launch the new product* |
| **leaflet** | *n* | 1 | a piece of paper containing information about a particular subject | The marketing department produced a leaflet to inform the public of the new product. |
| **life-cycle** | *n* | 3 | series of developments that take place in an idea or organization from its beginning until the end of its usefulness | Great things were expected of the new product but its life-cycle was quite short. *product life-cycle* |
| **liquidate** | *v* | 4 | to turn assets into cash | The company was liquidated because of its inability to get itself out of financial difficulties. *to liquidate a company* *liquidate asset* |
| **long-term** | *adj* | 4 | continuing for a long time or being effective for a long time | Hopes for a long-term solution to the problem are running high. *long-term solution* *long-term goals* |
| **margin** | *n* | 2 | a spare amount or degree of something | The company made a small profit margin on the product. *huge profit margin* *margin of profit was small/ huge* |
| **opportunistic** | *adj* | 3 | behaving in a way that involves taking advantage of a situation to make some gains | The company's opportunistic marketing policy ensured a huge profit. *opportunistic policy* *opportunistic move* |
| **oriented** | *adj* | 3 | directed toward a particular aim | The company is exclusively oriented toward profit and neglects the ethical dimension of the business. |
| **outstanding** | *adj* | 4 | still owing to someone | The business has outstanding debts of $20,000 and the bank has refused to give it a loan. *outstanding fines* |

| | | Unit | Meaning | Example |
|---|---|---|---|---|
| **oversee** | *v* | 1 | to make sure a job is done properly by watching people while they do it | One of the primary functions of a supervisor is to oversee the workers and make sure the job is done properly. |
| **penetrate** | *v* | 3 | to get into a particular area that is difficult | It took a long time but the company finally managed to penetrate the Chinese market.<br><br>*penetrate the market*<br>*penetrate the organization* |
| **personalize** | *v* | 3 | to make a subject or event personal by focusing on the individual or private concerns | By personalizing the argument, the employee was able to communicate the workers' issues to the employer. |
| **philanthropic** | *adj* | 5 | giving money freely to help other people who need it | The successful businessman set up a philanthropic trust to help people who suffer from malaria in Africa.<br><br>*philanthropic charity*<br>*philanthropic donations* |
| **pivotal** | *adj* | | vitally important | The decision to invest more money was pivotal in achieving the target set out by the business.<br><br>*pivotal role*<br>*pivotal decision* |
| **post** | *n* | 1 | a job or official position in a company usually involving some responsibility | She is well qualified for the post of Human Resources Manager and has been offered the job. |
| **potential** | *adj* | 1 | possible | There are potential markets and potential customers but we need to do research and target them.<br><br>*potential markets*<br>*potential customers* |
| **priority** | *n* | 1 | precedence in position | Priority must be given to the discussion of the budget for the launch of the new product. |
| **procedure** | *n* | 1 | a way of doing something, especially one that is formally accepted as correct | The proper procedure to be followed in making decisions is clearly laid out in the minutes of the meeting.<br><br>*follow procedure* |
| **proficiency** | *n* | 1 | ability or skill in doing something | The job of manager requires a great deal of proficiency in managing people. |
| **promotion** | *n* | 2 | a publicity campaign that is intended to increase the sales of something | The sales promotion was very successful and the product sold well.<br><br>*sales promotion*<br>*product promotion* |
| **prosperity** | *n* | 5 | condition of being successful | Since joining the Programming Department, Shane has enjoyed economic prosperity and security. |
| **prototype** | *n* | 3 | the first model that is made of something and used later as a basis for improved models | The prototype is very good but it still needs a lot of development. |
| **recession** | *n* | 4 | a period of time when the economy of the country is less successful, production is low, and unemployment is high | The country was hit by a recession and unemployment rose to 22%.<br><br>*hit by a recession*<br>*period of recession* |
| **regulatory** | *adj* | 5 | bringing into conformity with a rule, principle, or usage | The company relocated to an Asian country where the regulatory regime and taxation system are considered more attractive.<br><br>*regulatory body*<br>*regulatory system* |
| **reputable** | *adj* | 4 | being known for a good standard of work and service | He works for a highly reputable company that produces goods of the highest quality.<br><br>*reputable firm*<br>*reputable establishment* |

| | | Unit | Meaning | Example |
|---|---|---|---|---|
| **reputed** | *adj* | **5** | said or believed to be true | The new manager is reputed to be a workaholic. |
| **resilient** | *adj* | **3** | capable of not being damaged easily by being hit or stretched | The product should be made of a resilient material as it will be used on the sports field. |
| **retail** | *adj* | **2** | relating to selling goods to the public usually in small amounts or quantities | Positive retail sales data have driven the shares market up in a day of hectic trading. *retail price* *retail outlet* *retail figures* |
| **revenue** | *n* | **2** | the money that a company receives over a fixed period of time | The financial manager was very concerned about the drop in revenue from last month's high. *increase in revenue* *growth in revenue* *lost revenue* |
| **risk** | *n* | **1** | the act of doing something even though it may have unpleasant consequences or results | She took a risk and resigned from her job without the certainty of another position. *run a risk* *risk management* *be at risk* |
| **rock-bottom** | *adj* | **4** | relating to very low price or level | I bought these items at rock-bottom price *rock-bottom prices* *to hit rock-bottom* |
| **sample** | *n* | **3** | a small part of a larger group used to test ideas or get information about the whole group | The results are based on a random sample of the population surveyed over the last few months. *population sample* *market sample* |
| **screening** | *adj* | **1** | checking someone for security reasons | We need to find a company that can provide us with accurate and reliable screening services if we are to expand and hire more staff. *screening of employees* |
| **segment** | *n* | **3** | one part of a whole | A large segment of the population was affected by the increase in energy prices. *market segment* *profit segment* |
| **slump** | *v* | **2** | to fall suddenly and sharply | Profits slumped last year causing the company to reduce staff numbers. *demand slumped* *profits slumped* |
| **speculative** | *adj* | **4** | relating to risky activities in which goods are bought at a certain price with the hope of selling them at a higher price | The trading is purely speculative but we are hoping that the shares will yield a large profit in the future *speculative trading* *speculative property market* |
| **spiral** | *n* | **2** | a rise in cost that happens quickly and at an increasing speed | A wage and production cost spiral sent the cost of living out of control. *wage spiral* *price spiral* |
| **strategic** | *adj* | **3** | planning action(s) to achieve an objective | The chairman made a very strategic move in his bid to take over the company and he was successful. *strategic move* *strategic position* |

| | | Unit | Meaning | Example |
|---|---|---|---|---|
| **stringent** | *adj* | 5 | tightly and strictly enforced | More stringent controls need to be placed on imports from certain countries.<br>*stringent measures*<br>*stringent rules* |
| **subsidiary** | *n* | 5 | something that is less important than something else to which it is connected | This company is a subsidiary of a larger company but I think it could operate on its own.<br>*subsidiary company* |
| **survey** | *n* | 3 | a way of finding out the opinions or behavior of a particular group | The marketing department carried out a survey on the product potential.<br>*to conduct a survey*<br>*market survey* |
| **suspend** | *v* | 4 | to delay or stop something from being in effect for a while | All negotiations were suspended because of financial difficulties.<br>*suspend talks*<br>*suspend negotiations* |
| **sustainable** | *adj* | 3 | capable of being maintained or prolonged | Figures indicate that last year's unexpected growth in the airline industry is not sustainable due to the increase in fuel costs.<br>*sustainable development* |
| **target** | *n* | 3 | a goal to be achieved, for example, amount of profit expected | The sales figures indicate that we are right on target.<br>*reduce its price target* |
| **thriving** | *adj* | 5 | doing well and being successful | He is running a thriving business and making large profits.<br>*thriving company* |
| **transaction** | *n* | 4 | business that is carried out by two or more people negotiating about it | Business transactions can take a lot of time as everybody's point of view has to be considered and careful scrutiny of the proposals need to be ensured.<br>*financial transaction*<br>*cash transaction* |
| **turn-over** | *n* | 2 | a cycle of goods or sales during a particular period of time | The company has a turnover of about $10 million.<br>*annual turnover* |
| **universal** | *adj* | 5 | common to or proceeding from everyone in a particular group | There was universal agreement for the proposed merger though not everyone agreed on the terms.<br>*universal condemnation* |
| **verify** | *v* | 1 | to check that something is true by careful investigation | He was called into the meeting to verify the story of the new employee.<br>*verify a statement* |
| **volatile** | *adj* | 4 | subject to rapid change | The stock market can be very volatile in times of political uncertainty. |
| **voluntary** | *adj* | 3 | done of one's own will without being forced or paid | Attendance at the meeting was voluntary so numbers were low.<br>*voluntary work*<br>*voluntary subscription* |
| **workload** | *n* | 1 | the amount of work that has to be done by a person | Kien resigned because the workload was too heavy.<br>*heavy workload*<br>*reduced workload* |
| **yield** | *v* | 4 | to produce as return | The investment yielded a profit of 10%.<br>*yield a profit*<br>*yield returns on* |

# Audio Script

**Unit 1 Lesson 1**
CD
T-1 **Exercise b**

**Martha:** I think it's time we started thinking about our future and making decisions about what we want to do when we finish this course.

**John:** Oh, Martha, you're always so serious! We still have two months before we take our final exams.

**Martha:** I know, but you can't just suddenly wake up the day you finish college and find a job. You need to plan.

**John:** You're right, of course. But where do we start? The course we're taking is General Business and there are so many choices like Human Resources, Sales, Marketing, Finance, and so on. And I'm not even sure what I'm interested in.

**Martha:** Yes, I know. There's a lot to think about, but maybe we can start by thinking about our specific interests in Business. For example, I think that you should go into Marketing.

**John:** I've thought about that too, but I'm not sure. I suppose we should think about our different strengths and weaknesses in each area. A job in Human Resources or Management would probably suit you. You are bossy—you just love telling people what to do!

**Martha:** Hey, that's not true. It's just that I like organizing people and I think I'm pretty good at it.

**John:** Well, build on your strengths. I think we should also have a look at some ads and find out what kinds of jobs are out there in the real world.

**Martha:** Okay. Let's buy the newspaper every day this week and look at job ads in Business. We could also go to some companies and find out what skills and qualifications are needed for each department.

**John:** Good plan. I think maybe we should go see our college counselor too. She may have some useful advice for us.

**Martha:** Let's do that. I'll call her office tomorrow and see when we can get an appointment. I'll arrange for both of us to see her.

**John:** Great! I've got to hurry. I have a class in ten minutes. Bye.

**Martha:** Okay. See you later.

**Unit 1, Lesson 2**
CD
T-2 **Exercise c**

**PA:** Career counselor's office.

**Martha:** Good morning. Can I speak to Mrs. Mills, please?

**PA:** May I ask who is calling, please?

**Martha:** My name is Martha Willis. I'm a student at the university.

**PA:** I'm afraid Mrs. Mills is in a meeting right now. Can I ask why you are calling?

**Martha:** I need some advice on finding a job. Can I make an appointment to see her?

**PA:** Yes. When would you like to come in?

**Martha:** On Thursday afternoon if she is free.

**PA:** Let me check. Yes, that should be alright. Is three o'clock okay for you?

**Martha:** Yes, it is.

**PA:** Fine. So, that's three o'clock on Thursday the 15th.

**Martha:** Yes. Thank you. Oh, and can you also include my friend John Jones?

**PA:** Yes, that's no problem. See you on Thursday.

**Martha:** Thank you. Good-bye.

**PA:** Good-bye.

**Unit 1, Lesson 2**
CD
T-3 **Exercise f**

**Mrs. Mills:** Good afternoon, Martha and John. It's good to find students who are thinking about how to get a job.

Basically, it's a process and certain steps need to be followed. Let me take you through the most important ones.

But before we even begin we need to focus your search by matching your interests with your skills, abilities, personality, training, and qualifications.

Now, I see from your files here that you are both taking general Business courses and will graduate in June. The field of Business is very broad, so we need to think of your particular strengths and what you do and do not enjoy doing.

For example, if either of you likes working with and helping other people you would probably enjoy a career in Human Resources. The responsibility of the Human Resources employee is to match the person with the position. Recruitment can be done externally when a new employee is brought into the company or internally from within the company, which might involve promotion. The HR department also looks after staff development, welfare, and motivation. In other words, here you try to keep everyone happy.

Now if that's not you and you think you would enjoy the more aggressive side of the business world, there is sales and marketing. There your focus is the customer and convincing him to buy and for this kind of job you need to be tough.

And, of course, if you like precision and attention to detail, there is the world of finance. This kind of job includes the many aspects of calculating expenses, profits, revenue, and of course, investment.

You are going to have to give this some thought and not only about the jobs themselves, but the kinds of companies where you can work, which will make these jobs vary.

In the meantime, I can get you started on the form-filling, CV writing, and tips for interviewing. So shall we begin?

**Unit 1, Lesson 3**
CD
T-4 **Exercise h**

**Martha:** John, remember Mrs. Mills talked about strengths and weaknesses. I've seen those on applications and find it really hard to look at myself and decide what my strengths and weaknesses are.

**John:** I know, my brother said it's a matter of finding the balance between selling yourself and what you are good at, but not making yourself sound perfect. In other words, you need to be a bit critical of yourself without overdoing it. OK, so let's think and help each other out.

**Martha:** Well, John, I think you are really good at networking. You have a way with people and making contacts that I think would be very good in sales and marketing.

**John:** Wow, thanks, Martha. You're normally not so nice to me. As for you, I think your skills are organizational. You are very good at planning and seeing things through. This is definitely one of my weak areas. I think I'm just a bit lazy about getting myself moving.

**Martha:** Well, John, I don't think it's a good idea to tell a prospective employer that you're lazy. You can't completely hide the negative, but you need to put it in a more positive way. How about saying that you might be considered a bit disorganized, but that's because you focus on the communication side of the task and you're working on your organizational skills. As for myself, I could say that some people might say that I'm impatient, but this may be because I have a lot of drive and enthusiasm to get the job done. I still organize myself and check everything as I go along.

**Unit 1, Lesson 4**
*CD T-5*
**Exercise c**

**HR Manager:** Your resume is a very important document and with your application form and cover letter it's the employer's first introduction to you, and the measure of your suitability for the job. Remember that employers receive a lot of applications, so you have to make all your documents as readable and as user-friendly as possible.

The layout of your resume should be in a simple font, 11 or 12 point in Times New Roman or Arial script. Your contact details should be up-to-date and the e-mail address serious and not too much of an attention-grabber.

We generally advise people not to include age and marital status because some people object to being asked these questions. Likewise, you don't have to include information about your religion though sometimes this question may appear on the application form. It's advisable to include all information about your work experience, including temporary and part-time jobs since this will give the employer some insight into your background in dealing with customers and working as part of a team. Of course, give all relevant information about your education and include details on your involvement in sports and volunteer work, too, because this shows your personality. Of course, you should read the job ad carefully and follow the instructions given there. And make sure that you get approval from your references before including their names on your resume.

Any questions?

**Unit 1, Lesson 4**
*CD T-6*
**Exercise f**

**Manager:** Jane, what was your overall impression of the applicants?

**Jane:** I was impressed with both, but for very different reasons.

**Manager:** Yes, I agree. Applicant 1 has quite a lot of experience—overall 20 years, but is a little short in academic qualifications.

**Jane:** Yes, that's true whereas Applicant 2 has an M.A. in HR, and a very recent one, as well as a General Business degree. It's very important to have up-to-date theoretical knowledge.

**Manager:** You're right about that, but on the experience side don't you think she's a little weak?

**Jane:** Of course, but she's worked at that mortgage company,

which has given her some experience on the financial side of things whereas Applicant 1 has had more experience, but in more general situations.

**Manager:** True, but look at the wide range of responsibilities he's had in very important HR areas at management levels.

**Jane:** But we're looking for someone who's a team player and that's probably easier for a person who's new in the workplace. I wonder about the flexibility of a person who's been in management for so long.

**Manager:** Let's invite them both for an interview and keep these questions in mind as we're interviewing.

**Jane:** Good plan. I'll call them and make arrangements.

**Unit 1, Lesson 5**
*CD T-7*
**Exercise e**

**John:** Can I send an e-mail instead of a cover letter with my application?

**Teacher:** Yes, of course, if an e-mail address is included in the ad.

**Martha:** I know we use e-mail all the time and chat to each other, but can I use it in the same way for business communication?

**Teacher:** No, definitely not. There are certain rules you have to follow—we call it e-mail etiquette and it's important that you follow all these conventions.

**Martha:** Sometimes we don't use an opening greeting in our e-mails. Is that OK for business e-mail?

**Teacher:** You should always open with a greeting and end with a final salutation. When you don't know the person, use the same opening as you would for a letter, that is. Dear so and so . . . Make sure you add your signature at the end. If you're sending an e-mail to a colleague or friend you can just use the person's name.

**John:** What about length? I don't like reading from the computer screen and I hate it when I get a long e-mail.

**Teacher:** I think most of us feel like you, John. It's good to stick to one page—no more than a letter-sized page if printed out. You should use paragraphs as well. When you look at the cover letter you see it's divided into paragraphs—you should do the same on the e-mail.

**John:** Can I depend on the computer to do the spell-check and grammar-check?

**Teacher:** No, not really because, as you know, that feature is not always available on the e-mail program so make sure you check and edit it yourself. Remember also that it's OK to add gimmicky things like smiley faces when e-mailing friends and family, but never in a business e-mail.

**Unit 1, Lesson 6**
*CD T-8*
**Exercise d**

**Speaker:** Knowing how to prepare and behave is one of the keys to a successful interview. First impressions are based on appearance, so it is very important to pay attention to how you dress. Wear clothes that are fashionable, but appropriate and never show up for an interview in flashy loud clothing. This gives a very poor impression and possibly causes interviewers not to take you seriously. Remember, before you go to the interview do your homework and find out all you can about the company. Then when you go inside you can relax and be natural. Wait for the interviewer to invite you to sit down and be formal and polite in your opening greeting. Never say anything negative about a past employer even if you have had unpleasant experiences in your last job. Don't be afraid to keep eye contact with your interviewers and try to avoid giving short answers to questions. You can direct the flow of the interview by developing your answers.

## Unit 1, Lesson 6
**Exercise h**
CD T-9

### Interview 1

**Interviewer:** Have you checked out our company on the Net?
**Interviewee:** Yeah, there's a lot of stuff out there.
**Interviewer:** Were you impressed with what you read?
**Interviewee:** Yep, sounds pretty good.
**Interviewer:** Are you interested in working for us?
**Interviewee:** Yeah, I think so.

### Interview 2

**Interviewer:** What appeals to you about working for a company like ours?
**Interviewee:** Well, from what I have researched I think working with your company would be very challenging and would also give me the opportunity to learn and interact with experts in my field.
**Interviewer:** What kind of asset do you feel you would be to the company?
**Interviewee:** Well apart from the qualifications and experience that I have, I also feel that I am a highly motivated person who is capable of working in a team or alone.

### Interview 3

**Interviewer:** So, you're interested in joining our company.
**Interviewee:** Yes, that's right.
**Interviewer:** Do you know anyone who works in the company at the moment?
**Interviewee:** Yes, I have a couple of friends who are working here.
**Interviewer:** And what have they told you about the company?
**Interviewee:** That you are all very nice and helpful.

## Unit 2 Lesson 1
**Exercise f**
CD T-10

**Speaker:** In the traditional approach to selling, the salesman was someone who did it because he couldn't find another job. Selling often meant sticking your foot in the front door, bullying your way into a home, or conning the person into coughing up for a product that they may or may not need like a set of encyclopedias for the children. These days the image of the salesperson has changed drastically and a lot of preparation and psychology have gone into turning out a good salesperson. Still it does help if you have certain personality characteristics before you start. A person who's able to quickly pick up on the personality traits of another and build on this insight to create an emotional link is likely to succeed at sales. Such a salesperson recognizes the indecisiveness of a prospective customer and helps them make up their mind in favor of the product. It's important that the salesperson likes people and is able to tune into their different needs and wants. It's also important to be a good listener and pay attention to the value system of the customer. It's also a good idea to sell products that interest you as this makes selling easier.

## Unit 2, Lesson 2
**Exercise f**
CD T-11

**Salesperson:** Good morning. Can I speak with Geraldine Murray, please?
**Woman:** Speaking. How can I help you?
**Salesperson:** My name is William Cosgrave and I work for Telefast, a cost-cutting company that will reduce your phone bill by at least half. I hope this is a convenient time to talk.
**Woman:** Well, I am a little busy right now . . . What's it about?
**Salesperson:** Oh, I'm sorry. I hope you received the brochure we sent out on how to cut your phone bills in half.
**Woman:** No, I didn't receive anything, but if there's a genuine way to help reduce my phone bills, count me in. Can you give me a quick explanation?
**Salesperson:** Certainly. It's quite simple. I can send you information on the different deals that we offer. If you're interested, just complete the application form and send it back. We have a special offer if you sign up this month. For just $6.99, you get all local calls free for one month and after that a 50% reduction on these calls. And if you make international calls at off-peak times, there is a 40% reduction and a 25% reduction at busy times.
**Woman:** Hmm . . . that sounds interesting. How do I sign up for this?
**Salesman:** Just give me your address and I'll send out the information today. Remember, if you want the free calls for a month, you need to apply right away. Can I just check that I have your correct address?

## Unit 2, Lesson 3
**Exercise f**
CD T-12

**Speaker:** Today, I am going to give you some advice regarding what to do and what not to do when giving a presentation. It's important to remember that though your purpose is to inform and share with your audience, you should select what they can comfortably deal with in a single sitting and not overload them with minute details. The next thing you must ensure is that you arrive organized for your presentation with your notes in order. The content should be organized in a logical way and you should inform your audience of this layout in your introduction. Make sure you do not wander into asides and unrelated comments. Stick to the main point. Also, it's important to establish a good rapport with the audience and to make eye contact with your listeners. Don't shout or whisper, but speak clearly and loud enough for everyone to hear. Keep your voice at a comfortable speed. Finally, conclude by summing up the essential points and then ask if anyone has any questions.

## Unit 2, Lesson 3
**Exercise g**
CD T-13

**Presenter #1:** Hi, everyone. Good to see you all here and thanks for coming along. I hope you will find my topic interesting and not boring. Okay, let's start, shall we? Can you all sit down and listen, please? Right now, where are my notes? Hmm . . . they're in a bit of a mess. Hang on a minute while I get organized.
**Presenter #2:** Good afternoon, everyone! Welcome and thank you for coming along to the presentation. Today, I would like to look at some recent trends in the sales of organic produce, especially through supermarket outlets. The talk will last about forty minutes and then we will have about ten minutes at the end for discussion, so please save your questions until then.

**Presenter #3:** So, we've looked at how the Organix Company got started and we have considered one of their principal achievements. Before considering their other two important accomplishments, let's take a quick look at the management structure of the company. Now does anyone have any suggestions as to what those two other accomplishments are?

## Unit 2, Lesson 4
CD T-14
### Exercise a
**Kathy:** Good morning. Furniture Wholesalers. Can I help you?

**Benson:** Hi. This is Craig Benson here from Hooliers Hotel.

**Kathy:** Oh, hi, Mr. Benson. How are you? It's been a while.

**Benson:** Yes, hasn't it? I think it's been over a year since we talked. How's business?

**Kathy:** Very good. We've expanded. We opened a new warehouse about six months ago and took on five new employees.

**Benson:** That's great! I hope you are not too busy to fill our order. We've expanded also and need lots of new furniture.

**Kathy:** Oh, that's great. So how can we help you?

**Benson:** Well, first I need to know if we can have a rush on this order since it's coming up to summer. We need to have it delivered before May 15.

**Kathy:** I'll have to check with deliveries. Let me know what you need and then I'll get back to you.

**Benson:** Fine. Right, let's see—10 double beds, 20 single beds, 30 closets and matching dressers. That'll do for now but I think we'll also need some dining room furniture.

**Kathy:** Okay, that's 10, 20, 30, and 30. Let me call you back in an hour or so after I've checked delivery availability. Then I can get all the details for delivery if it is possible.

## Unit 2, Lesson 4
CD T-15
### Exercise b
See dialog above.

## Unit 2, Lesson 4
CD T-16
### Exercise e
**Sales:** . . . so, I'll need to set up a new account for you, especially if you say that you want to become a regular customer. First of all, let me have the name and address of your business.

**Buyer:** Okay, the name of the restaurant is Totally Natural and the address is 43 Riverside Way, Delham.

**Sales:** Delham . . . Right, that's just inside the limit of our delivery service. Now just give me an account number that we can use for all our transactions. With this number, it'll be easy to find your account details each time you call.

**Buyer:** I see. Okay, let's use 1979. It's easy to remember as it's the year I was born.

**Sales:** Okay. We put TF in front of that, which stands for Truck Freight. So, when you call, please quote TF-1979, which is your purchase order number. Now what can we prepare for you today?

**Buyer:** Today we need 5 pounds of cauliflower, 10 pounds of potatoes, and 8 pounds of onions.

**Sales:** Right. That, according to our codes, is 5 x #05, 10 x #04, and 8 x #02. Items will be delivered first thing tomorrow morning.

## Unit 2, Lesson 5
CD T-17
### Exercise b
### Situation 1
**Customer 1:** Hi, I was in your store last week and I bought myself a jacket. I wore it for a few days, but I really didn't like the color. I'm wondering if I can exchange it or get my money back.

### Situation 2
**Customer 2:** Good morning. I'm calling about the digital camera that I bought yesterday. When I tried to use it today the zoom lens didn't work. I'd like to return the camera and get a replacement or talk with someone who knows something about the camera who can perhaps guide me through the process.

### Situation 3
**Customer 3:** Hi, there. I just picked up a TV at your store yesterday afternoon and when I was taking it out of the car it sort of accidentally fell. It looks okay, but the picture is pretty fuzzy. Do you think I can have someone look at it or get a replacement or a refund?

## Unit 2, Lesson 5
CD T-18
### Exercise e
### Situation 1
**Customer:** Good afternoon. I would like to speak with the manager, please.

**Salesperson:** Why? What's your problem?

**Customer:** Well, I bought this DVD here three weeks ago and have had several problems with it in that short time. Each time, I bring it back here, someone looks at it, adjusts something, and says it's okay. But then when I get home it doesn't work.

**Salesperson:** Hmm . . . Are you sure you know how to operate this machine?

**Customer:** Young man, I've been a customer at this store for several years and no one has ever spoken to me like this before.

**Salesperson:** Okay, okay. I'll get someone to have a look at it.

### Situation 2
**Customer:** I'm returning this jacket because it's not really the right fit and it's sort of heavy.

**Salesperson:** I'm very sorry, sir, but that jacket was bought during the sales and the store policy is no refunds on goods bought during sales.

**Customer:** Oh, be reasonable! It's just a jacket. I'm sure you still have some others inside. Surely you can exchange just one jacket?

**Salesperson:** Sir, it's impossible. Our policy clearly states "No exchange on sale items." I can't do anything to help you, I'm afraid.

**Customer:** Oh, this is ridiculous! I'm never going to shop here again!

### Situation 3
**Customer:** I just bought this new TV and when I got home it didn't work.

**Salesperson:** Okay, if you could wait a moment, I'll have someone look at it.

**Customer:** Look, I have been waiting for five minutes! I can't stand here all day. I have to get back to work. Listen to me. I need this TV to be fixed right now or I need a replacement!

**Salesperson:** Please stop yelling. The service manager is busy right now and so you'll have to wait.

**Customer:** I'm not going to put up with any more of this. Call the manager right now!

## Unit 2, Lesson 6
### Exercise e
CD T-19

**Speaker:** The Internet has expanded our choices of where and when to shop, but it also has its hazards. Here are some things that you should think about before becoming an Internet shopper.

It is safer to buy from reputable companies, so do a little research on the company before making your purchase. Check carefully all the contact details of the company. Look for a street address and a landline telephone number, not just an e-mail address. Also, consider any extra costs—things like shipping costs and taxes—that you may have to pay and decide if it's actually worthwhile buying online.

Generally, people pay for online goods with credit cards. Make sure that the site is secure. At the bottom of the page, you should see a small "s"—which stands for "secure"—along with a picture of a padlock. Make sure you keep copies of the order form and the acknowledgement notice that you receive.

When you buy online, you have the same legal rights as when you buy in a store. However, it's very important to read all the terms and conditions of the sale before you buy.

Always check your bank statement after making a purchase and make sure that only the amount that you paid has been deducted from your balance.

Each country has its own consumer affairs offices that should be able to advise you if you find that you have been cheated while shopping online. The most important thing to remember is "If in doubt, don't buy."

## Unit 3 Lesson 1
### Exercise e
CD T-20

**Speaker:** Companies advertise their products for three main reasons. The first reason is simply to inform the public that a particular product or service exists. This type of advertisement gives factual information about a product, provides price details and information about any special offers. This is called informative advertising and it concentrates on just giving the essential details. It's often used to give information about household products that people buy regularly.

The second type is persuasive advertising and its function is to convince people to buy a product or service. The advertisement tries to achieve this by telling people that the product or service will bring beneficial changes to their lives. This often happens with cosmetic products where a person is persuaded that a certain face cream will rid them of wrinkles and make their skin look fresh and young. Services like cosmetic surgery work on the same principle.

The third type of advertising is known as competitive advertising because the purpose here is to convince people that a particular company's products or services are better than any other produced by its competitors. In some countries, companies are allowed to mention their competitors by name in their advertising. In other countries, this is not permitted.

## Unit 3, Lesson 2
### Exercise c
CD T-21

**Speaker:** Branding, like marketing, is as old as the concepts of ownership and selling. In former times, people branded an item simply to show who the owner was and, of course, this is still one reason behind branding. In the past, a mark was placed on the ear of a sheep or cow to identify the owner. In the same way, the earliest craftsmen put a simple mark on a product to show ownership. This was often just the craftsman's name, in the same way that a painter still signs a painting. The marketplace was somewhere you went to get your practical needs and the sign or brand indicated the person who could satisfy those needs.

In the 21st century, brands are more likely to signal the availability of a product, but their role has changed quite a lot. While still indicating where a product can be found, the scope of the brand is much wider now and is often associated with certain qualities the product may have. In addition, certain brands have become status symbols, particularly among young people. This can be seen in all kinds of goods such as sportswear, shoes, T-shirts, and even in services where a hotel brand does not indicate just a bed for the night, but a whole host of associated luxuries.

## Unit 3, Lesson 3
### Exercise e
CD T-22

**Speaker:** Good morning, everyone. Well, I think we are all clear by now about the importance of knowing as much as possible about potential customers and possible competition from other companies when we set out to market a new product. Today, I want to look at the different ways we collect data. We want to find out all we can about consumers' income, likes, dislikes, and where they live. We also need to investigate our competitors' prices and methods of advertising.

There are two ways of getting this information. The first is through primary research and this involves getting out there and talking to people. We prepare a questionnaire that considers the likes, dislikes, and income levels of consumers, and we try to find out what newspapers and magazines they read. This information can also be gathered via a phone interview. We can also make note of what shoppers buy when they go out as well as using television panels where consumers and retailers give feedback.

The other type of research requires less physical effort and is often referred to as secondary research. Sales reports and trade figures are analyzed for existing information. Magazines, newspapers, and government publications as well as Internet searches provide useful data. So let's consider some of these in more detail . . .

## Unit 3, Lesson 4
### Exercise c
CD T-23
## Company 1

**Speaker #1:** Joe Mason, a computer programmer, hit upon a very marketable piece of software almost by accident. Along with his wife, Alice, he set up a company to market software that facilitates online photo sharing. Since its launch, the program has attracted interest from organizations that want to include it on their Web sites. The Masons have adapted the software so that it can be installed on other Web servers and have begun to sell licenses.

## Company 2

**Speaker #2:** A major software manufacturer is about to launch its new operating system. It has already launched a major marketing campaign with the aim of convincing people to line up at retail stores in anticipation of the product on the morning of its launch. The company has already convinced a celebrity talk show host to include their product on her list of favorite things, and it hopes that, through this massive campaign, within two years over 400 million users will be using its software.

## Company 3

**Speaker #3:** Televised sporting events have become big business. At the 1996 Olympic Games in Atlanta, a leading sportswear company conducted a successful and relatively inexpensive advertising campaign for their products. Instead of paying the official $50 million sponsorship fee, it plastered the city with billboard ads, gave out free banners to spectators, and set up a huge promotion center near the principal stadium knowing that all these things would inevitably appear during broadcasts of the event.

## Company 4

**Speaker #4:** Many of the people who use a company's free e-mail service become, in one way or another, involuntary advertisers for that company. The number of users of one of the leading free e-mail services grew from zero to twelve million in just eighteen months. Since then, numbers have increased to over 100 million users. Ads appear in e-mail messages with the apparent "endorsement" of the sender and they reach a potentially huge number of e-mail users.

### Unit 3, Lesson 4
### Exercise d
CD
T-24 See the text above

### Unit 3, Lesson 5
### Exercise b
CD
T-25 **Tom:** I hate these monthly meetings! They are just a waste of time even though I know it does give us a chance to talk things over face to face. Today I have a lot of work on my desk.

**Monica:** Well, you do have a point, Tom, but I think meetings do help us clear up some ambiguous issues that might be troubling people. You have to admit that in this company management is very fair and through these meetings they keep us well briefed on new proposals and developments.

**Tom:** Well, I guess you're right. I've worked at other places where staff is never included in decision-making but that's certainly not true here and we do have lots of opportunities to give our feedback.

**Monica:** I'm glad you're coming round to seeing the benefits, Tom. Remember also we get a chance to be involved in the planning stages and input our views on the whole process.

**Tom:** Okay, got it, but these meetings always come at a bad time for me when I have lots of work going on.

### Unit 3, Lesson 5
### Exercise f
CD
T-26 **Steiner:** Lisa, I'd really like to get this agenda ready and out to the staff by tomorrow morning. Can you type it up for me, please?

**Lisa:** Certainly, Mr. Steiner. Could we just run through the items that you want me to include?

**Steiner:** Well, the first thing is to get the minutes of the last meeting out of the way and any questions that might crop up from those.

**Lisa:** Don't forget that there are two new staff members to

be introduced.

**Steiner:** Yes, that's important. Thank you for reminding me. We'll welcome them immediately after the apologies for absences.

**Lisa:** Right. Okay, I've got all that.

**Steiner:** Well, that takes care of the formalities. Now the main points of business . . .

**Lisa:** I suppose the first item will be organizing the marketing research?

**Steiner:** Well, no, not quite yet. I'd like to discuss financial matters first with a brief outline of budgetary considerations.

**Lisa:** I see.

**Steiner:** Next, we should look at target markets and forecasts for sales.

**Lisa:** So, where should I put the market research?

**Steiner:** That's next followed by a discussion of a timetable for research and analysis.

**Lisa:** Okay. And we finish up with Any Other Business, right?

**Steiner:** Right. So, Lisa, can you take care of it from here? Please let me know when you've distributed it to the staff.

**Lisa:** Certainly, Mr. Steiner.

### Unit 3, Lesson 5
### Exercise g
CD
T-27 See dialog above.

### Unit 3, Lesson 6
### Exercise c
CD
T-28 **Speaker:** The violation of intellectual property rights and the illegal copying of all kinds of goods from cigarettes to medicines really took off in the 1990s and has become an issue of major concern to companies and governments around the world.

Counterfeiting is worrying multinationals as it now makes up between 5 and 7% of all global merchandise trade, giving rise to $512 billion in lost trade annually. The World Health Organization says that about 10% of the world's medicines are counterfeit.

### Unit 3, Lesson 6
### Exercise d
CD
T-29 **Speaker:** Here are some examples of the kinds of fake goods that have been found in the marketplace. A woman in New York recently phoned her local drugstore to complain about the bitter taste from the cholesterol-lowering Lipitor pills that she was taking. On examination in a lab, the pills turned out to be counterfeits. Over the next two months, 16.5 million pills were withdrawn from warehouse and pharmacy shelves resulting in a huge loss to the company.

A tip-off in Brazil led to the discovery of a large number of bogus Hewlett-Packard printer cartridges ready for the marketplace. Police also picked up information from the same source that led to the seizure of more than $1 million worth of other counterfeit goods.

In a Chinese warehouse, authorities came across a store of counterfeit Buick windshields ready for the export market. China also sells Honda fake parts for half the price of the original.

Secret service agents in Guam discovered bogus North Korean-made pharmaceuticals, cigarettes, and counterfeit $100 bills.

French Customs recently picked up more than 11,000 fake parts for Nokia cell phones, batteries, and phone covers.

## Unit 3, Lesson 6
### Exercise e

**T-30** **Speaker:** And the list goes on and on. What can companies and governments do to control this violation? China is by far the greatest violator of property rights and two-thirds of the world's fake goods are turned out there. However, the Chinese government, under pressure from international groups, is now beginning to clamp down on illegal copying. As Chinese companies begin to experience violations of their copyrights from within China they are starting to demand more regulations. In addition, multinational companies are putting pressure on the governments of violating countries to make them control the counterfeiters. Goods are being electronically tagged and companies are sending detectives around the world to track down companies and countries involved in the production of fake goods.

## Unit 4 Lesson 1
### Exercise b

**T-31** **Roger:** Hi, Michelle. How are you doing?

**Michelle:** Hi, Roger.

**Roger:** So, are you ready for the independent life?

**Michelle:** Well, you know how I was really looking forward to getting away from home? Well, now I'm beginning to wonder how I'll manage my money and survive on my own. It's easy when your parents pay all the bills but it's gonna be different from here on.

**Roger:** Yeah, I know. My rent is $400 a month and that's in a shared house.

**Michelle:** Mine is the same, but that includes all bills.

**Roger:** Really? Not for me. I have to pay all utilities separately—it'll be about $50 a month. My parents are going to pay for my tuition this semester—about $500.

**Michelle:** Mine too—I think it costs the same as yours. You know, I think the toughest thing to manage is going to be food. There's always the temptation to eat fast food, but that is so unhealthy. I am going to try to follow a healthy diet. My mom thinks food will cost about $100 a week.

**Roger:** I want to keep my food expenses down to about $70 a week. I am also going to buy a bike and cycle to college. That way I won't have any transportation expenses.

**Michelle:** My accommodation is only a five minutes' walk from the college so transport expenses will only be train fares home, which is about $50 a month.

**Roger:** I bought enough clothes for the term, so I don't really expect to have to spend anything on clothes.

**Michelle:** Same with me. You know, I heard books can be quite expensive. We might have to spend like $300 on textbooks!

**Roger:** That's a lot! I'm going to try to find some used books. I'd like to keep the cost of books to around $150. And what about recreation? I definitely need to go to the movies like at least once a week. I'm going to budget for about $30 at first.

**Michelle:** Me, too, and then a little more after I find a part-time job. Anyway, I've got to hurry now. See you tomorrow.

**Roger:** Yeah. See you, Michelle.

## Unit 4, Lesson 1
### Exercise d

**T-32** **Anne:** Doing an MBA is definitely expensive. I need to prepare a personal budget. I should plan my expenses so I don't end up broke in the middle of the year. First, I'll calculate my expenses so I can figure out how much I'll have for the year. It's a good thing I worked in the summer—the $2,500 I managed to save will definitely be useful along with the $1,000 I have in my savings account. I think I can count on about $250 a month from my part-time job at the library so that gives me another $2,500 for the year. I really don't want to take any money from the family, but they have agreed to cover any medical and dental expenses—hopefully there won't be any. Then there is the $1,000 from the grant along with payment of the tuition fees, which is a great bonus. I think I'll go ahead and sell my car. I won't need it this year and that should get me another $2,000.

## Unit 4, Lesson 1
### Exercise e

**T-33** **Anne:** Right, now the hard part—expenses. First thing every month is the rent—$400 a month. I'll have to stay in the shared house because I just can't afford a place on my own. Books and supplies it seems will cost about $300 in total and I'll probably need about $350 a month for food and household supplies. I'll definitely have to cut out shopping for new clothes and limit myself to about $50 a month for entertainment and let's say $40 a month for phone and just $20 for transportation since I can walk to most destinations.

So, if my calculations are correct, that gives me $9,000 income and expenses of over $11,000 so I'll need to borrow to deal with the difference. I'll go to the bank early next week and request a loan of $3,000. I can defer payment until I graduate. I'd better find a good job after this!

## Unit 4, Lesson 2
### Exercise f

**T-34** **Bank employee:** Good morning. Can I help you?

**Chris:** Yes. My name is Chris Brown. I have an account here and I'd like to apply for a credit card.

**Bank employee:** Fine. Can you give me your account number and let me check your history with us?

**Chris:** Here it is. I've had an account here for the last four years.

**Bank employee:** I see. Well, from what I see here, Chris, your credit history is good—just one small loan that was paid back on time. Of course, you know that as a student there are some restrictions on the type of credit card you can have.

**Chris:** Yes, I'm aware of that. But I really need a card for booking airline tickets and things like that.

**Bank Employee:** Okay, well, the first thing to do is fill out this form. Then I have to give it to the manager for his approval. But that shouldn't be a problem.

**Chris:** Great. Now, can you explain about the different repayment options that are available?

**Bank employee:** Certainly. You can choose to make a partial payment each month on what you owe on the card, or you can pay the balance in full each month, or you can pay a fixed amount in equal payments at fixed intervals. Personally, I would recommend making a partial payment each month on what you owe.

**Chris:** Fine. But what about the charges and interest rates on the card. I've heard that they can be quite high.

**Bank employee:** Our bank charges a fixed annual charge of

$40 for using the card. If you don't pay the minimum amount due within the given time limit, the interest rate here is 18%. The most important thing is to pay off the minimum amount due on time.

**Chris:** Okay, well let's set it up so that the minimum amount due is automatically deducted from my checking account.

**Bank employee:** Certainly. So, if you could just fill out this . . .

### Unit 4, Lesson 3
CD T-35 **Exercise c**

**Finance Director:** The company's fixed assets consist of buildings worth 400,000 dollars, various types of equipment with a total value of 50,000 dollars, and motor vehicles that are worth 60,000 dollars.

Our current assets include stock worth 7,000 dollars plus 2,000 dollars in cash. We are also owed 5,000 dollars by various debtors.

As for current liabilities, we still have an overdraft of 2,500 dollars and we owe 800 dollars to various creditors.

### Unit 4, Lesson 4
CD T-36 **Exercise c**

**Speaker:** In the period from February to March, the following price changes were noted:

The price of milk went up from a dollar fifty to a dollar sixty a quart while the price of an 18-ounce container of yogurt stayed the same at two dollars and fifty cents.

The price of a loaf of bread increased slightly from three dollars to three dollars and five cents.

Sugar also went up in price from one dollar a pound to one dollar and five cents.

The price of apples saw a twenty-cent increase. A pound cost two dollars in February and two dollars and ten cents in March.

Tea also went up. The price of a box of 100 tea bags went from two dollars twenty to two dollars thirty cents.

The only item to go down in price was coffee. An 18-ounce can cost four dollars in February and three dollars and fifty cents in March.

### Unit 4, Lesson 5
CD T-37 **Exercise c**

**Investor:** So, what can you tell me about the different options for investing my money?

**Expert:** Well, there are a number of things you can do. Let's start with stocks and shares. The obvious advantage here is that you can make a lot of money quickly. But on the down side, you can lose all your money, including the principal. It can be risky.

**Investor:** I see. What about a more low-risk investment?

**Expert:** Okay. Well, there are a couple of options here. You can invest in bonds. With bonds, you are guaranteed the return of your money along with promised interest payments. There is no risk. Of course, the disadvantage is that the returns are not very high. The same is true with other fixed interest investments. As with bonds, there are low levels of risk and guaranteed returns on your investment. But the returns are low and, generally, your investment is tied in for a fixed period of time.

**Investor:** What about property? Is that a good thing to invest my money in?

**Expert:** It can be. With property, there is the possibility of high returns. And it is a relatively safe investment as property generally holds its value. And you can borrow against the value of the property. One drawback is that you may have to spend money on the maintenance of the property. Its sale value will depend on its location and on the property market at the time of the sale.

**Investor:** I've heard of something called "index futures." What can you tell me about them?

**Expert:** Ah, yes. Well, here there is the possibility of making large profits if prices move in the direction that you anticipated. Of course, you need to be well informed. Success depends on your ability to predict the direction of demand.

### Unit 4, Lesson 6
CD T-38 **Exercise c**

**Speaker:** Hello, everybody. I'm here to give you some information and advice about online trading in stocks, securities, etc. so that you can maximize your profits as an online trader while at the same time protecting yourself.

The first essential step is to find out all you can about trading online before you begin. Do your homework as you would for any other type of investment that you plan to get involved in.

Before you start, do comparative studies of the kinds of service available and when you have found a broker make sure that he or she is trustworthy by carrying out a safety check. This can be done online.

You should find out what happens to your order after you have placed it. Bear in mind that you shouldn't expect instant placement just because you've sent the order to your broker. Don't be impatient. Wait for confirmation that your order has been received or you may find yourself placing the order twice.

As for how much you are prepared to invest, well my advice is to set yourself some sort of limit. Be aware that the market price may take you into a range of prices where you hadn't intended to go.

### Unit 5 Lesson 1
CD T-39 **Exercise e**

**Speaker 1 (from China):** When I first came to the USA, everything was very strange. In China, people generally do not express their opinions so openly. We like to talk, but we are more reserved about our own opinions. I found American people very outspoken and so used to expressing themselves. I felt inadequate at first and I was scared to open my mouth! I was surprised at the way students challenged their professors and how employees argued with their bosses. At first it seemed to me like a lack of respect for their superiors, but now I know it is normal. I also found the humor strange in the beginning and I could never understand the jokes. But I'm adjusting to that and even beginning to laugh at some of the jokes.

**Speaker 2 (from the UK):** When you're in Saudi Arabia, it is very important to follow all the social and dress conventions. I always wear a long-sleeved shirt and often a jacket as well — even in the stifling heat. If my Saudi host removes his shoes going into a building, then I have to do the same. I have to remember to never point at anybody and under no circumstances eat with my left hand. Another thing I have to remember is not to sit with the sole of my shoe or my foot exposed.

**Speaker 3 (from Japan):** Now I'm used to the Brazilian way of doing business, but it took some time. In Japan, we like to plan ahead so setting up appointments a couple of weeks in advance is not a problem for us. However, what we do find strange is the way Brazilians touch you on the arm or on the back while talking to you. We Japanese are much more formal than this and a lot of physical contact in public is not our style. Also, Brazilians are more relaxed and they tend to spend fifteen minutes or so on small talk before starting a meeting. I find this a bit of a waste of time, but we have to observe their customs. I used to find it frustrating but, you know, it does help to get to know people and the meeting then usually runs more smoothly.

**Speaker 4 (from the USA):** I find that many French people are very conscientious about dress and so I have to make a bit of an effort because I think we Americans are more casual. Sometimes I find it a bit stifling because I like to take my jacket off and roll up my sleeves when getting down to business. The French don't do that, so I have to keep my jacket on in meetings. One thing that I find a bit irritating is the French attitude toward time. Compared with many Americans, they are quite casual about their timekeeping so I don't try to pack too much into one day. For me, one of the biggest challenges has been improving my French. They definitely like you to try to speak the language even if you can't conduct the whole meeting in French.

**Speaker 5 (from the UAE):** I find that Australian society is much more casual than Arab society. People dress in a very casual manner even in the workplace. What is probably most different for me is the Australians' punctuality as this is not one of the strong points of my culture. Australians also like to maintain strong eye contact and this can sometimes make Arab people feel uncomfortable. Australians are friendly but they are also very direct and we are not used to this. In our culture, we like to preface business deals with small talk and inquiries about the other person's health and general chitchat. But Australians prefer to get right to the point.

**Unit 5, Lesson 2**
**Exercise b**
CD T-40
**Dave:** I used to think that it would be great to work in an open work environment and—don't get me wrong—there are many positive aspects to this kind of working environment. I find a lot of stimulation and motivation in communicating freely with a variety of ideas and hearing all the interesting ideas that come up during the day. The challenge of being involved in decision-making does keep you on your toes. However, the downside is that the physical open plan is often not so conducive to concentration. I find it difficult sometimes to get a lot accomplished because of the constant buzz and hustle and bustle around the place.

**Marcia:** When I went for the interview for my current job, I was completely overwhelmed by the approach of the Managing Director. We were a group of ten candidates interviewing for five positions. They put us all together in a room and then when the MD walked in, he had a football under his arm. He tossed it to someone without saying anything. Afterwards, I realized that he was assessing two things – our reaction to a new and different approach and our ability to operate as a team. Now that I understand the MD's approach, I really

appreciate his ability to think logically, but also laterally.

**Omar:** I really like my job, I mean the actual work that I do because it is very challenging and I get to learn a lot. But the organizational culture of the company frustrates me very much. I know it's the type of system I grew up in where those at the top controlled everything and made all the decisions. However, I have outgrown that and I feel that as a professional I should have the chance to give some input into decision-making even if it is just to give my feedback on what is happening. I want more say and I wish that not all authority was in the hands of just a few.

**Unit 5, Lesson 2**
**Exercise f**
CD T-41
a. A much more flexible approach to management . . .
b. Traditional business structures are changing . . .
c. Nowadays, companies need . . .
d. However, greater stress levels have developed . . .
e. A new trend called convergence has recently emerged . . .
f. Telephone calls can be recorded and saved . . .
g. With the arrival of wireless technology, . . .

**Unit 5, Lesson 3**
**Exercise b**
CD T-42
**Marcus:** If I had the choice, I think I'd choose to work from home. I work for a high-tech company and there are certain times in the month when I'm under a lot of pressure to meet deadlines and then there are other times when I'm just sitting around with very little to do. But I have to come in and spend eight hours a day here at the office irrespective of the workload. If I worked at home, I could balance my work time to match the workload.

Of course, there could be some complications working from home, I mean, things like powerful and reliable network connections, which are guaranteed at the office, but which might be more uncertain at home.

**Paula:** I work in Human Resources and, of course, a lot of my work is office-based. But I'd like to have the choice to do some work from home. I have two young children and it would be helpful if I could work from home sometimes, particularly when they're at home sick. The other advantage of working from home is that I could eliminate the time that I spend commuting in the rush hour.

On the other hand, there are definite advantages to working at the office. I have access to all the resources I need and, of course, in my work face-to-face meetings are very important.

**Jake:** My name is Jake and I'm a manager at a large software company and I can see the advantages and disadvantages of having people work from home. The company would certainly save money if some employees worked from home. We would save on office space, energy, security, and cleaning. We could just arrange some space when we need to get together for meetings.

However, I have some reservations too. For example, it would be difficult to monitor and control people's work output and, of course, employees could have problems keeping the network up and running. I think we still have some way to go before we can have people operating from home, but I'm willing to experiment.

**Unit 5, Lesson 4**
**Exercise b**
CD T-43

**Speaker:** Enron Corporation was an American energy company based in Houston, Texas. Before its bankruptcy in late 2001, Enron employed around 21,000 people and it was one of the world's leading electricity, natural gas, pulp and paper, and communications companies. Its claimed revenues in 2000 were $101 billion.

*Fortune* magazine named Enron "America's Most Innovative Company" for six consecutive years, from 1996 to 2001. Enron also appeared on *Fortune's* "100 Best Companies to Work for in America" list for 2000.

The Enron bankruptcy was the biggest in U.S. history to that date and it cost 4,000 employees their jobs.

**Unit 5, Lesson 5**
**Exercise e**
CD T-44

**Businessman:** Before we even get to the product itself, we have to think about labor costs, especially in terms of outsourcing production to a cheaper location. After we've dealt with these concerns, we get closer to the production and marketing costs. In this industry the cost of raw materials is a factor though nowadays we have a lot of synthetic fabric and so these costs can be controlled better. Probably more important than raw material costs are marketing costs. These include surveys to gauge new fashion trends and changes in people's tastes. Then we have to consider the competition and that also takes time and money. Inflation is not such a major concern these days as it is pretty much under control. Our production costs are more affected by health and safety regulations and by pollution control as we have to invest quite a bit of money into these two areas.

**Unit 5, Lesson 5**
**Exercise f**
CD T-45 See text above.

**Unit 5, Lesson 5**
**Exercise h**
CD T-46

**Businessman:** As people involved in business, I think our greatest concern is the cost of energy. Think about it—in the mid-90s, oil was around $11 a barrel. Oil-producing countries felt they were giving away their black gold for next to nothing. But just over a decade later, the price has increased by 700% and income for the producers has increased accordingly. Of course, the price of oil is not an isolated thing. It's very much tied up with politics and more recently, as we saw in New Orleans, with the weather. These are factors that you might think are not immediate concerns for businesspeople, but these days they're very much on our minds. At the end of the twentieth century,

oil was at a reasonable price of around $25 a barrel but events like September 11th seriously affected prices driving the price to $50 a barrel for the first time ever. Over the last five years, a combination of political crises and weather factors—particularly storms—have driven the price to unprecedented highs of $72 a barrel.

**Unit 5, Lesson 6**
**Exercise c**
CD T-47

**Speaker:** Ethical companies are usually set up by people with certain beliefs and principles. The aim is to be profitable and to give people what they want, but without compromising these principles. These companies usually have strong beliefs regarding such issues as chemicals, organic food, the environment, animal testing, fair wages, and child labor.

In the late 1990s, many investors, especially venture capitalists, began shouting for a return on their investments. For many of these ethical companies, going public was not a viable option. At the same time, the large multinationals saw the amazing growth and interest in organic and ethically traded goods. It was cheaper for them to buy an existing established ethical company than to set up their own.

**Unit 5, Lesson 6**
**Exercise d**
CD T-48

**Speaker:** The Body Shop is a cosmetics company that was set up by Anita Roddick in the 1970s. What made it different from so many other cosmetics companies was that it did not deal in products that had been tested on animals. Recently, the Body Shop was sold to L'Oreal, a very large French company that doesn't adhere to the same principles as the Body Shop. Another product that followed the "no animal testing" principle was Tom's of Maine, a small company that makes toothpaste and other cosmetic and hygiene products, but it too has been bought by a much larger company, Colgate.

A number of vegetarian and organic food companies that followed their principles strictly have also sold out to larger companies that may not adhere to the same principles. Linda McCartney's Whole Foods has been bought out by Hain Celestial while Ben and Jerry's Ice Cream has been taken over by Unilever.

Two other well-known companies that have also sold out are Green and Black's Chocolate, bought by Cadbury-Schweppes, and the Odwalla and Samantha juice companies, acquired by Coca-Cola. Stonyfield Farm Organic Yogurt, which always used organic milk in its products, has been acquired by the French company Groupe Danone.